GREAT
SHARK
STORIES

edited by
VALERIE and RON TAYLOR
with Peter Goadby

BOOK CLUB ASSOCIATES LONDON

First published in 1978 by Harpers & Row Publishers, Inc.
in association with The K.S. Giniger Company, Inc.

This edition published 1987 by
Book Club Associates
by arrangement with The Crowood Press

Printed and bound in Great Britain by
Mackays of Chatham Ltd

Contents

Foreword iv

Introduction 1

I Stars of the Silver Screen 7
1 From *Blue Meridian:*
The Search for the Great White Shark
by Peter Matthiessen 9

2 The filming of *Blue Water, White Death*
by Valerie Taylor 16

3 From *Jaws*
by Peter Benchley 25

4 The Filming for *Jaws*
by Valerie Taylor 34

5 Filming Tiger Sharks
by Valerie Taylor 42

II Shark Behaviour 47
6 From *Sharks, Sea and Land*
by 'Sinbad' 49

7 From *Lord of the Sharks*
by Franco Prosperi 55

8 The Vanishing Grey Nurse
by Valerie Taylor 60

9 From *The Arcturus Adventure*
by William Beebe 66

10 From *Sharks and Other Ancestors*
by Wade Doak 71

11 Great White Death
by Valerie Taylor 79

III Scientific 90
12 'Sharks that Ring Bells' from
The Lady and the Sharks
by Eugenie Clark 91

IV Divers and Sharks 106
13 From *The Coast of Coral*
by Arthur C. Clarke 108

14 From *Men Beneath the Sea:*
Conquest of the Underwater World
by Hans Hass 113

15 The Mesh Suit Experiment
by Valerie Taylor 126

16 Riding a Shark
by Valerie Taylor 130

V Sharks that Attack 134
17 From *Sharks and Shipwrecks*
by Hugh Edwards 137

18 From *Shark Attack*
by H. David Baldridge 143

19 From *About Sharks and Shark Attacks*
by David H. Davies 151

20 From *Shark Attack*
by Victor M. Coppleson 154

21 From *Sharks and Rays of Australian Seas*
by David Stead 160

22 From *The Shark Arm Case*
by Vince Kelly 164

Foreword

Among the many rewards the book *Jaws* bestowed on its creator was the opportunity to meet and work with some of the legendary figures in the small and dedicated shark fraternity, including the team that filmed what remains perhaps the finest underwater documentary ever made, *Blue Water, White Death*: producer/director Peter Gimbel, Stan Waterman and the exquisite Taylors, Ron and Valerie.

The first and lasting impression I had of Ron and Valerie is that they defy the macho mystique. They are quiet, genteel, devoid of bluster and braggadocio, not only reluctant to toot their own flutes but almost compulsively understated about their extraordinary lives. They'd never say this, but I will: they seem to personify Hemingway's definition of courage – grace under pressure.

I suppose that their manifest modesty, which is neither false nor theatrical, comes in part from a conviction that to avoid aggrandizing their own accomplishments is one way to encourage others to regard sharks in a proper perspective. Ron and Valerie are fervent opponents of the public's penchant to monsterize this majestic natural predator.

And I suspect that they have ambivalent feelings towards *Jaws* the book, which was as accurate as I could craft it, and *Jaws* the movie, which was inevitably afflicted with Hollywood hyperbole, for both creatures *did* monsterize sharks while for the first time making the public aware that sharks were both more and less than their nightmares fancied.

Great Shark Stories is part of the Taylors' ongoing crusade to reduce myth to fact, to tell the truth about sharks. If some of the tales seem fantastic, don't dismiss them: they are all true. One of the book's many virtues is that the Taylors have demonstrated that the truth about sharks is spectacular enough. Sharks don't need a boost from fiction.

As I write this, I'm preparing to go diving with the Taylors in far New Guinea. I have in hand a note from Valerie in which she says that she's tempted to bring along her steel-mesh shark suit. It might, she muses characteristically *sotto voce*, come in handy.

Oh-oh . . .

PETER BENCHLEY
Princetown, N.J.

Introduction

About ten years ago, a survey was conducted in Australia in an attempt to establish which word had the greatest impact on the largest number of people.

Researchers tested words like rape, death, murder, sex, love, snake, poison. To their surprise, it was the word *shark* which aroused the public's emotions more than any of the others.

At the time, I thought that it must have been because of the large number of attacks that have occurred in Australian waters, for Australians are very conscious of sharks.

But I realize, now, that Australians are not alone in their hatred and fear of sharks. The film *Jaws* brought forth an almost universal reaction against these large fish. They had, to most people, been a distant threat, not likely to be encountered at the local beach, but in the wake of the film a type of mass hysteria seemed to grip whole communities and once popular beaches were almost deserted.

Men took to the oceans armed with shark-catching equipment. The old saying, 'The only good shark is a dead one,' became a new law. Around Australia, great sharks were slaughtered by the hundreds for their teeth, most of which were sold in the United States for up to twenty-five dollars each.

An American promoter offered one million dollars to an Australian diver to swim into a steel cage with a great white shark. He was to kill it with an explosive-tipped spear while the TV cameras rolled and the world watched. I believe that there would have been very little danger involved. The diver would probably have had to swim around in front of the shark to make it look exciting.

Trapped sharks have only one desire – to escape. Sharks, particularly large dangerous ones, don't take kindly to living in captivity and are, generally, already half dead on reaching a holding tank. As for starving the shark to make it more dangerous sharks can go happily for months without eating.

The whole thing must have sounded like a bad joke to anyone who knew anything about sharks and their behaviour. To the general public, though, it seemed that the diver was brave and probably more than a little mad to even contemplate such an impossible task.

Fortunately, this little piece of stupidity has not taken place and although, at the time of this writing, still planned for the future, seems doomed to failure, simply because it will be so difficult to find and keep alive a shark suitable for the stunt.

My husband, Ron, and I have worked with sharks in their natural element for over thirty years and, without intending to, we have acquired a reputation as shark experts. 'Shark expert' – it sounds very important, but it is hardly an apt description. So little is known about the sharks that inhabit our oceans that I don't think there is anyone who can justly claim the title.

A scientist who works with a certain species of shark over a period of years would become an expert on that particular species, but could hardly be called an expert on sharks in general. Ron and I know, from observation, a certain amount about a dozen different types of shark. Of the other two hundred and fifty or so species we know very little, or nothing. This hardly qualifies us as experts.

Our main claim to fame is the work we have done with the great white shark, *Carcharodon carcharias*, the fish that ate its way to worldwide hatred in *Jaws*. The interest aroused by Peter Benchley's book and the later film brought us a continuous flood of mail. Selling shark pictures became big business for us, and we had plenty of them.

Books and magazines devoted to sharks and their habits flooded the market. I walked into a big bookstore in Sydney recently to see no less than seventeen recent publications on sharks staring down at me from the shelves. Nine of them had a photograph taken by us on the cover, two of them without permission or payment. Some of these books were excellent, but most were full of exaggerated, often false, accounts of shark attacks. It doesn't matter, the public laps them up – the more gore the better.

What is this sea creature that seems to have captured the imagination of so many people so completely?

Sharks were an ancient species when the dinosaurs walked the earth. They outlived the dinosaurs as they did countless other creatures that evolved, multiplied, dominated, then vanished, leaving only fossil remains to let us know that they ever existed at all. Yet, through all this time, sharks prospered. Their unique bodies were so well designed that there appears to have been very little change in their shape since prehistoric times.

Most sharks are not dangerous to man. Some do not have teeth in the true sense, but hard, bony crushing plates, suitable for grinding and eating shellfish. Others feed on the smallest creatures in the sea. Many do not grow longer than a few feet. Of the larger sharks considered dangerous to man, only about ten species have been known to attack without provocation.

Of these, only members of the family Carcharinidae (whites, whalers, Zambezi, bull) and the tiger shark attack man on anything like a regular basis. In the Caribbean there have been reports of unprovoked attacks by the hammerhead shark, but throughout the rest of the world this species seems to be innocent of any unprovoked aggression towards man.

The key to many attacks is provocation. Any shark, even one without teeth, will try to defend itself if hooked, speared, or otherwise molested. This is perfectly normal; any living creature, man included, will do the same.

When assembling stories for this collection I found many books on sharks to contain identical information presented in different styles, although often the conclusions drawn by the various writers differed widely. In any case it made selection limited. But, eventually, with the help of many people, I arrived at a final choice.

One thing that stands out in the final selection is how differently two people can think about a shark. A great deal of this has to do with the circumstances of the contact, but, even so, the variations of opinion are amazing and interesting.

If I seem to favour stories about skin divers and sharks, I guess it is only natural. As a professional diver, I feel that accounts of a man or woman, often armed with nothing more than a camera, confronting a potentially dangerous shark in its home, make exciting reading.

I am often asked why sharks attack people. This is a difficult question to answer, simply because there are probably as many reasons as there are shark attacks. Dr H. David Baldridge, in his book *Shark Attack*, states that approximately 4 per cent of all shark attacks are due to hunger. That leaves 96 per cent which must have other causes. The reasons for some are apparent. Most obvious is a shark attacking a diver who is spearing fish.

A bleeding, struggling fish is the natural prey of a shark, which will move in very quickly for the kill. Usually, when it sees a big, ungainly creature already in possession of its potential prey, the shark will leave. Some may hang around, in which case it is wise to stop spearing fish.

On rare occasions the shark attacks. A very hungry shark, following the scent of blood or the vibrations of a dying fish, would quickly fall into a feeding pattern. This means that it has made up its mind to eat even before seeing the food source.

It would seem that once you have seen the shark, the chance of attack is slight. It may be significant to note that few divers have ever seen the shark before it attacked except in cases of provocation. I have been bitten on three occasions. Each time there was food in the water as well as on my person.

I was provoking the sharks into a feeding pattern. One of the bites was a definite attempt to eat a portion of my body, one accidental, in other words, both the shark and myself made a mistake, and one a fast terrifying warning hit to the face that left me dazed and bleeding. Fortunately I was wearing the mesh suit at the time and only four teeth penetrated just under the chin, but the shark, a grey reef, came with such speed I was unaware of what was about to happen.

Only once have I had trouble with a shark after I had been watching it. It was one of a pack of about twenty. All the other sharks were circling at a respectful distance, except for one bad-tempered female. She circled close, faster and faster ignoring the baits on the sand. I knew what was coming and braced myself. Suddenly she sped straight at me, and just before she struck, her jaws and pectoral fins dropped. I rammed my camera into her mouth, and after about 30 seconds (it seemed like hours) of mad punching, kicking, and yelling, my companion speared her in the gills.

This may indicate another reason for attack, a shark which is mad, an observation that F. A. Mitchell-Hedges also makes in his book *Battles with Giant Fish*. I have seen thousands of sharks, but only one which behaved in this way. The water was very clear, so it was not a case of mistaken identity, which may often be the case with swimmers or waders in dirty water, such as is found in harbours and estuaries. Here the shark is unable to see because of poor visibility. There may be something in the water which upsets its sense of smell, perhaps human urine. It may then bump or bite the object merely to discover what the obstruction is. Sharks don't have hands and have to feel with nose or teeth. If the object is a human leg, we have a shark attack. This theory gains credibility from the fact that in these types of attacks, the victim, though mauled, is rarely, if ever, eaten. Personally, I would never go swimming in dirty water which is adjacent to an ocean.

Before shark meshing reduced attacks on surfers off Australian beaches (there has never been an attack on a meshed beach), every summer saw a number of unfortunate incidents involving sharks biting swimmers. Some victims were just bumped or cut by fins, some lost limbs and others lost their lives. A possible reason for this type of attack could be that the shark is just swimming along in a normal fashion and suddenly finds itself among a lot of large, unusual creatures. Not having experienced this type of situation before, the animal may panic. During that panic, it would bump anything hindering its escape to open water and may even bite it.

I am also asked why a shark will single out a swimmer in the centre of a crowd. This question is almost impossible to answer. I don't really think that a shark has any more reason for selecting one individual from a large crowd than a bird has for eating one grape from a bunch or a human for taking a particular egg from a carton. It is just one of those things. But once a shark selects a victim and continues the attack, it is almost always on the same person. This is true of most carnivores. A cheetah will run past a dozen impala before bringing one down. If the first attack only wounds and the impala escapes, the cheetah will continue after the wounded animal, regardless of the number of others nearby.

Surfboard riders, waiting for a wave with their legs hanging down on each side of the board, look very vulnerable from beneath. A shark with even a slight amount of curiosity must feel compelled to investigate. If I were a surfboard rider, I would paint two mean-looking eyes on the bottom of my board. Sharks don't like being looked at. An eyeless object would possibly be worthy of inspection and perhaps a nibble by a passing shark.

The sharks that I have been writing about up to now are the whalers, Zambezi, bull sharks, and their cousins. These are the sharks responsible for most of the attacks on humans. However, there is one shark which is quite different, the 'Great White Death'. Great white sharks have different personalities and behaviour patterns than all other sharks. They are the end of the food chain.

Whites eat almost anything. Nothing eats a white shark, except a bigger white shark, but even these huge fish don't swim around attacking everything in their paths. They choose their prey as nature intended they should, from the slow, the sick, and the old. I hate to say it but, in the water, a human looks very much like a slow, old seal. These mammals are one of the staple foods of the great white. What appears to be an unprovoked attack by a white could well be brought about by the awkward movements humans make when swimming.

All this is just theorizing. I do know that some species like certain colours; some sharks are attracted to unusual vibrations and smells; some are attracted by specific patterns. All that I can say with certainty is that sharks are predictable only in that they are unpredictable. Each different attack could be caused by a different reason or they could all be triggered by similar causes. I don't know. No one really knows. There are so many variables that to go into them all would require a book twice this size and even then we wouldn't know.

What can you do if menaced by a shark? I can only repeat the advice that I give my nephews when they go out on their surfmats. I make them put the blue side down. I won't let them swim in dirty water or on a rising tide during the late afternoon. I have told them that if they are ever in the water with a shark that appears menacing to put their heads under the water (even without a face mask) and look at the shark. They may not be able to see the shark very well, but the shark doesn't know that. Having your dinner look you in the eye can be disconcerting, and for sharks, it is worrisome. They are not accustomed to this sort of reaction when they approach. Being animals which work on instinct, not reason, it generally becomes difficult for them to make a decision.

Anything which keeps the shark off-balance is a help. If contact is made, make as much noise as possible. Punch and kick, especially at the eyes and gills; this seems to act as a deterrent in many cases. Everything should be tried. Fight, don't just give in and let the shark do as it pleases.

VALERIE TAYLOR

1 Stars of the Silver Screen

The best-known shark movies ever made are Peter Gimbel's documentary *Blue Water, White Death* and Zanuck-Brown's *Jaws*. Both had a shark as the main attraction. There the similarity ended as far as the finished product was concerned. 'Bruce', of *Jaws* fame, was a giant mechanical monster, while the white shark in Gimbel's film was the much smaller real thing. My husband, Ron, and I were fortunate enough to work on both these films and for us, as far as the filming went, there was little difference. Our job was to film live great white sharks for both *Jaws* and *Blue Water, White Death.* The same locations were used on both occasions and, for all we know, even some of the sharks could have been the same.

Great whites appear to have territories in which they hunt, and the same sharks could have very easily visited the filming locations for both films. Although the location, method of attracting sharks, and the time of the year were similar, Ron was required to shoot quite different film actions. In *Blue Water, White Death,* everything is shown as it happens. Everybody involved appears on film. Much is made of the cages, baits, boats, and people on board.

When filming for *Jaws,* all those things were still present, but they could not be shown. The shark was not supposed to be swimming around our boat and cage off Dangerous Reef, Australia, but trailing a different boat on the other side of the world, near Martha's Vineyard. This made filming much more difficult because sharks don't follow a script. Ron would feel himself lucky if he managed to shoot two or three scenes in a day without getting any of our gear in the picture.

More recently, we were required to film great white sharks for the Dino De Laurentiis production *Orca.* Once again, cage bars were not allowed in the picture. This was, by far, the most difficult filming job we have ever attempted. The script was simple enough and all arrangements were normal, but the shark never came in to perform. Week after week, we waited without completing our filming. A great deal of money was spent with very little return. Dangerous Reef did not live up to its reputation as the home of the great white shark. With one exception, the few sharks we did attract performed poorly or did not perform at all.

Professional shark fishing coupled with big-game fishing for great whites had taken its toll. Dangerous Reef, at the time of this writing, can no longer be considered a sure thing for anyone who wants to film or observe great white sharks.

Fortunately, the great white sharks of Dangerous Reef still live, on the silver screen. They have been seen by more people in more countries than any other shark in the world. Their fame is, without doubt, widespread. *Blue Water, White Death* and the *Jaws* films have made great whites the most famous sharks in the world and, unfortunately, the most feared.

1

From *Blue Meridian: The Search for the Great White Shark*

Peter Matthiessen

Reading Peter Matthiessen's words takes me straight back to the time when we were working with those fine Americans on the film *Blue Water, White Death,* sharing with them sad and happy days in pursuit of the great white shark.

It was the highlight of my life. Nothing I have done before, or since, has meant so much to me.

Blue Water, White Death did not turn out to be a million-dollar home movie, as Matthiessen feared – it is the best underwater documentary ever made. It will be a long time, if ever, before anyone else produces a comparable film.

Peter Matthiessen, in his book *Blue Meridian,* tells of the film from its beginnings in New York to the final shooting at Dangerous Reef, off the South Australian coast.

He tells of the time spent waiting for sharks which never came; of the fruitless five months spent crossing the Indian Ocean; of the despair when the producers thought that the shark would never come; of the elation and excitement when one finally did appear. This excerpt describes the sighting of the first white shark.

Ron and I never doubted that the waters of Dangerous Reef would provide all the shark action Peter Gimbel longed for. We had filmed there before and all that we needed was patience.

Since Matthiessen wrote *Blue Meridian,* between twenty and thirty rare great white sharks have been caught in this area. They have been taken not because of man's fear of a silent killer lurking in the depths, but to satisfy a fad, caused by *Jaws,* of wearing a shark's tooth around the throat. Great whites have become profitable.

Dangerous Reef has become a place of death not only for the great white but for our charter vessel, the *Saori,* too, which was later beaten to pieces against the cliffs of Wedge Island, within sight of the Reef. The last time I was there, her remains could still be seen protruding above the surge.

■

On the radio this morning one of the tuna captains with a white-shark charter party out of Port Lincoln had some disturbing news: in his last three trips to Dangerous Reef he had raised only one shy white shark, and it would not come near the boat.'Not like it used to be,' the radio voice said. 'They're being slowly killed out, I reckon, like everything else in the world.' This man blamed the gill-netters for the disappearance of the sharks and certainly commercial netting is a factor. Like other large predators of land and sea, the white shark will not survive long without the protection that it is unlikely to receive from man, and possibly the Australians are correct in the opinion generally held here that the species is nearing extinction. I am happy that our expedition has no plan to kill one except in self-defence.

There are recent reports of white sharks farther north in the gulf and to the west of Cape Catastrophe, and there is a feeling aboard that the *Saori* should pursue these sightings. Pursuit might relieve the strain of waiting and improve morale, but chasing works no better with fish than it does with anything else; better to pick one likely place and chum the hell out of it, day and night. By the time the slow *Saori* got the cages to the scene of any sighting the shark might be twenty miles away, and even if a shark were present, there is no guarantee that water clarity would be adequate, or that the shark would approach the cage. Possibly inshore sharks have a hunting circuit, moving from point to point as wolves do, but more likely they move at random taking prey as chance presents and congregating now and then at likely grounds like Dangerous Reef. Instinctively, I agree with Captain Arno, who is relieving Captain Ben over this weekend. Arno is a wonderful bent old salt with white broken bare feet that never sunburn; offered grog, he smites the table, crying out fiercely, 'I will!' Says Arno, 'Sharks have a head and a tail, and they keep swimming. Nobody knows where the shark goes. I reckon they don't know where they are themselves.'

Although these days are painful for Gimbel, they are almost as hard on Rodney Fox, who must choose the fishing grounds and baiting techniques that will bring the missing sharks. Rodney performs his duties with efficiency and style, but his casual air of cocky indifference is deceptive. If anything, he takes too much of the burden upon himself, and tends to construe the discussion of alternatives as implied criticism. For those aboard with a long interest in the sea and sharks, such discussions are fun and ease the strain, but giving a hearing to amateur opinions is hard on Rodney's nerves in a nervous time. Rarely does he permit the strain to show but sometimes, muttering 'Too many cooks ...!' he lies face down on the deck, feigning deep sleep, and one day he actually took refuge in the hold, refusing to come out to eat his lunch.

Nevertheless, Rodney says, he has never worked with a nicer

group of people. I feel the same, and so does everyone else; even Lipscomb and I, who often disagree, manage to disagree in a friendly manner. After a year and a half, this film crew is truly a unit, and its strength is mutual affection and acceptance; each man knows precisely what can be expected of the man beside him and demands no more, because those who fail in one respect have made it up over and over in others. As relationships have grown, the people have become more self-sufficient. Even the hearts game, a loud nightly event aboard the *Terrier*, has given way to books and chess and backgammon.

There are other changes, in the crew's youngest members especially. A new confident Cody is so loose that he threatens to join the extroverts while Lake has arrived at a new awareness in his dealings with others. One day on the deckhouse, watching for sharks, Peter said, 'Remember when I wrote you that I didn't really care about this film? Well, that's all changed – I do.'

By now everyone cares about the film quite apart from his own investment in it, if only because everyone cares about Peter Gimbel, who has his life's work on the line. A great part of the suspense of waiting for 'Big Whitey', as the near-mythical ruler of these silent seas has become known, is the knowledge that his failure to appear could be fatal to the film. Therefore the ship is quiet. Against these stark horizons, even the throb of hard rock music has a thin, tinny ring.

More than once I went ashore and prowled the tide pools. I have spent hours of my life crouched beside tide pools, watching the slow surge of simple organisms still close to the first pulse of life on earth. On Dangerous Reef are gaudy giant limpets, and companies of blue, black, and banded periwinkles, and the green snail and a brown cone and a very beautiful cream volute with zigzag stripings; also rockfish and the great fire-coloured rock crabs that grow enormous in the deeps, and a heart-coloured sea anemone, and a garden of hydroids, barnacles and algae. In every tide pool the seal pups played, and others lay on the warm rocks in a sleep so sound that they could be petted without awakening. When at last one did come to, it would stare for seconds in bare disbelief, then bleat in dismay and flop away at speed over the rocks.

In the white surge along the shore, the seals rolled endlessly, turning and twisting, whisking clean out of the water in swift chases or ranging along, the sleek, sunshined dark-eyed heads held high out of the sea. A small surge would lift them out onto the granite where, groaning, they dozed on the hot rocks in rows. The old bulls, though graceful in the water, were less playful; they stationed themselves on underwater ledges like old mighty sentinels and let the white foam wash around them. Onshore, competitors were driven off in heaving neck fights that were mostly shoving contests; the animals swayed their heavy heads and necks in the way of bears, to which among land mammals they are most closely related. Sea lions are agile on the land and a golden-maned bull protecting a cow and a new pup drove me up onto high ground. One cow was raked drastically on her hind end and right hand flipper by the parallel black lines of an old shark bite, and it was noticeable that the young never left the shallows and that even the adults kept close to the reef edges when not off at sea.

At noon today the *Sea Raider* brought word that an eleven foot white of thirteen hundred pounds had been hooked at Cape Donington, where the *Saori* had anchored two nights before. Psychologically this news was painful, but the water clarity at Cape Donington is awful and we could not have worked there. And at least it was proof that the species were not extinct.

In a letter to a friend this morning, Valerie wrote that no shark had been seen, but that she expected a twelve- or thirteen-footer to turn up at about 2:00. At 2:20 Peter Lake and Ian McKechnie saw a fin in the slick, some fifty yards behind the ship: the spell was broken. We dragged on diving suits and went on watch, but the fin had sunk from view in the still sea. A half hour passed, and more. Then, perhaps ten feet down off the port beam, a fleeting brown shadow brought the sea to life.

Suspended from a buoy, a salmon was floated out behind the boat to lure the shark closer. Once it had fed at the side of the boat, it would be less cautious; then, perhaps the engine could be started and the cages swung over the side without scaring it away. But an hour passed before the shark was seen again. This time a glinting rusty back parted the surface, tail and dorsal high out of the water as the shark made its turn into the bait; there was the great wavering blade exactly as Al Giddings had described it and the thrash of water as the shark took the salmon, two hours to the minute after the first sighting when Stan Waterman cried, 'Holy sweet Jesus!' – a very strong epithet for this mild spoken man; he was amazed by the mass of shark that had been raised clear of the water. Even the Australians were excited, try as they would to appear calm. 'Makes other sharks look like little frisky pups, doesn't it?' cried Valerie with pride. Then it was gone again. Along the reef a hundred yards away, the sea lions were playing tag, their sleek heavy bodies squirting clean out of the water and parting the surface again without a splash, and a string of cormorant, oblivious, came beating in out of the northern blue.

Gimbel, annoyed that he had missed the shark, was running from the bow; he did not have long to wait. From the deckhouse roof, I could see the shadow rising towards the bait. 'There he is,' I said, and Rodney yanked at the shred of salmon, trying to bring the shark closer to the ship. Lipscomb, beside me, was already shooting when the great fish breached, spun the sea awash and lunged after the skipping salmon tail; we stared into its white oncoming mouth. 'My God,' Gimbel shouted, astounded by the sight of his first white shark. The conical snout and the terrible shearing teeth and the dark eye like a hole were all in sight, raised clear out of the water. Under the stern, with an audible whush, the shark took a last snap at the bait, then wheeled away; sounding, it sent the skiff spinning with a terrific whack of its great tail, an ominous boom that could have been heard a half-mile away.

For a split second there was silence, and then Lipscomb gave a mighty whoop of joy. 'I got it!' he yelled. 'Goddam it, I got it!' There was a bedlam of relief, then another silence. 'Might knock that cage about a bit,' Rodney said finally, hauling in the shred of fish; he was thinking of the baits that would be suspended in the cage to bring the shark close to the cameras. Gimbel, still staring at the faceless water, only nodded.

Just after 5:00 the shark reappeared. The late sun glistened on its dorsal as it cut back and forth across the surface, worrying a dead fish from the line. There was none of the sinuous effect of lesser sharks; the tail strokes were stiff and short like those of a swordfish, giant tuna, and other swift deep-sea swimmers. This creature was much bigger than the big oceanic sharks off Durban, but for a white shark it was not enormous. Estimates of its length varied from eleven feet, six inches (Ron always plays it safe and underestimates, said Valerie) to fourteen feet (Peter Gimbel: 'I saw it alongside that skiff and I'm certain it was at least as long – I'm certain of it!'), but much more impressive than the length was the mass of it, and the speed and power. 'It doesn't matter what size the bastards are,' Rodney said. 'A white shark over six feet long is bloody dangerous.'

The day was late. In the westering sun, a hard light of late afternoon silvered the water rushing through the reef, and nearer the blue facets of the sea sparkled in cascades of tiny stars. More out of frustration than good sense, the choice between trying to film the shark immediately and trying to lure it to the baits alongside, in the hope of keeping it nearby overnight, was resolved in favour of immediate action. The motor was started up and the cages swung over the side, and the cameramen disappeared beneath the surface. But the great shark had retreated, and did not return.

By dark the wind exceeded 25 knots, and went quickly to 30, 40, and finally, toward 1:00 in the morning, to 50 or better – a whole gale. On deck, I lay sleepless, rising every little while to check the position of the light on Dangerous Reef. The reef is too low to make a windbreak, and even close under the lee, the *Saori* tossed and heaved under heavy strain. But Captain Ben, who knew exactly what his ship would do, slept soundly below. Towards 3:00 the wind moderated, backing around to the south-east, where it held till daybreak.

This morning the wind has died to a fair breeze. Waiting, we sit peacefully in the Sunday sun. The boat captains handline for Tommy-rough, a delicious small silver relative of the Australian 'salmon'. Others tinker with equipment, play chess and backgammon, write letters and read. Peter Lake has put a rock tape on the sound machine, and on the roof of the pilothouse, overlooking the oil slick, I write these notes while listening to The Band. Onshore, for Jim Lipscomb's camera, Valerie in lavender is baby-talking with baby seals, and I hope that most if not all of this sequence will die on the cutting-room floor. Unless it points up the days of waiting, such material has no place in the climax of the film; it will soften the starkness of this remote reef as well as the suspense surrounding the imminence of the white shark. Stan and Valerie, with a background of lecture films and a taste for amateur theatrics, share Jim's appetite for 'human-interest stuff', which might yet reduce this film to the first million-dollar home movie.

Towards dark another shark appeared, a smaller one, much bolder. Relentlessly it circled the ship, not ten feet from the hull. On one pass it took the buoyed tuna at a single gulp.

Since it passed alongside, the size of this shark could be closely estimated: all hands agreed that it was between nine feet and ten. But if this was accurate, the shark yesterday had been larger than thought. Rodney now said that it was over twelve, Valerie between thirteen and fourteen, and Gimbel thought that it might have been sixteen feet: 'I thought so yesterday,' he said, 'but I felt foolish, with everyone else saying twelve.' I thought thirteen feet seemed a conservative minimum. In any case, it had twice the mass of tonight's shark, which was plenty big enough. As it slid along the hull, the thick lateral keel on its caudal peduncle was clearly visible; the merest twitch of that strong tail kept it in motion. Underwater lights were lit to see it better, but this may have been a mistake; it vanished, and did not return the following day.

On January 26 the *Saori* returned to port for water and supplies. There it was learned that four boats, fishing all weekend, had landed between them the solitary shark that we had heard about on Saturday. The *Saori* could easily have hooked two, but what she was here for was going to be much more difficult. Meanwhile, a sighting of white sharks had been reported by divers working Fisheries Bay, west of Cape Catastrophe on the ocean coast, where three whites and a number of bronze whalers had been seen schooling behind the surf; the bronze whaler, which may be the ubiquitous bull shark, *C. leucas*, is the chief suspect in most shark attacks on Australia's east coast.

On the chance that the shark school was still present, we drove out to the coast across the parched hills of the sheep country. Over high, wind-burnt fields, a lovely paroquet, the galah, pearl grey and rose, flew in weightless flocks out of the wheat; other paroquets, turquoise and black and gold, crossed from a scrub of gum trees and melaleuca to a grove of she-oak, the local name for a form of casuarina. Along the way were strange birds and trees in an odd landscape of wind-worn hills that descended again to the sea-misted shore. From the sea cliffs four or five whalers were in sight, like brown ripples in the pale green windy water, but the white sharks had gone.

2

The Filming of *Blue Water, White Death*

Valerie Taylor

On 4 May 1969, Ron and I began what was to be one of the most exciting two days we have ever experienced. Had the events that I wrote about not been substantiated by the film *Blue Water, White Death*, I would have been hesitant to submit the story for publication. It all seems so incredible. This action was recorded near the beginning of the filming, when we were following the whaling fleet out of Durban, but to Ron and me it was the highlight of the six months we spent on the film.

Although, in the finished production the great white sharks were considered to be the stars, it was the oceanic whitetips which were responsible in my opinion for our most dangerous and exciting moments.

Even now, seven years later, I can still close my eyes and fill my mind with that blue, bottomless ocean full of grey torpedo shapes circling, ever circling.

I can see the dead whale floating in a cloud of blood. I can see my companions, ugly awkward shapes surrounded by the deadly beauty of a hundred sharks. I can see our whale catcher, the *Terrier VII*, silhouetted on the surface far above.

I feel sure that each of us there was driven by a different need ... I know that if I had said that I was afraid, that I didn't want to do it, not one person would have criticized, but the thought never crossed my mind: I did what they did, even though I felt that we would probably be killed.

The excitement of what we planned to do was all-consuming. It left no place for fear or misgivings.

This segment from my diary is part of a much longer story from an unpublished book. I believe it to be the ultimate in shark adventure. It is nothing to do with my writing – it's just the events that happened as I put them down at the time.

The men with whom I shared this experience are still my dear friends and I think of them often with the affection and respect that can only come from the sharing of a profound experience, each relying on the other with complete faith.

I consider myself lucky and my life richer because of this adventure 80 miles from the South African coast, under the Indian Ocean.

■

A.M.

We have just dropped off yesterday's whale completely unused at the flencing station, and are now looking for another. Unfortunately the weather is still awful – overcast, squalls, and rough seas. Poor Peter Gimbel, he has so many problems without worrying about the weather.

Later P.M.

Things improved rapidly during the day. The wind dropped away, the sun came out and we found a whale with sharks. There was still a heavy swell running, but I prefer a swell to a short chop. I watched as the cages were lowered. There was less fuss than usual. The whale was bleeding well. How sad it looked in death! Another innocent victim of man's greed.

Peter Gimbel had worked out a plan of action for us divers. I was to try to swim among the sharks while Stan, Ron and Peter filmed not only me but each other. Peter also wanted extreme close-ups of the sharks feeding.

We went down in the cages. The plan worked very well until halfway to the whale. Suddenly, as if on call, the sharks lost interest in the whale on which they were feeding, and became overwhelmingly attracted to us. We were completely surrounded by the grey marauders as they converged upon our tight little group, bumping and nuzzling.

From every direction they came. I was conscious only of myself, my companions, and the sharks. All else in the world was forgotten. I beat them off furiously with the powerhead, hitting the eyes and jabbing the gills with all my strength.

Peter, Stan, and Ron kept their cameras rolling. There was no need to look for the action; it was everywhere. I thumped and whacked as fast as I could. Stan said afterwards, he filmed a giant shark nuzzling my head. I remember feeling my hair being pulled and looking up to see an ugly snout and gaping jaw directly over my head. The sight gave me quite a shiver. I am glad someone filmed it.

Part of Peter's plan was to film, in close-up, sharks feeding on the whale, but we never made it. The sharks beat us back every time.

Ron finally killed, with his own powerhead, one shark that persistently came too close. It died a beautiful death, shuddering down in ever-decreasing circles, bumping several of its comrades in the process. Both Stan and Peter filmed this action.

We ran out of film and air after what seemed a very short time and returned to the *Terrier VII* for more of both. It was warm on the deck and I savoured the noisy crew working around us, but within 15 minutes we were all back with the sharks and into the action again.

This time, for some reason, the sharks were definitely less aggressive. I wanted to test my powerhead and tried my hardest, without success, to kill one. I had been given a different powerhead than what Ron and I normally use in Australia and although I left an indentation on the shark's head, and once took a piece right out, the thing refused to detonate.

Via sign language, I was told all the things I was doing wrong but was rather pleased when Peter Gimbel, trying the same stunt, using my powerhead, met with similar success. (It was later discovered the cartridge was wet, so I didn't feel too badly).

Finally, between us all we must have hit the whole fifty or sixty sharks at least once because one hard look, a shake of the fist, and they would shy away, rolling their eyes and jamming their gills tightly shut. Peter got all the shots he had planned except close-ups of the sharks feeding. They did get some film of sharks swimming into the blood and hitting the whale, but clarity was poor and the action confused.

The magazine in Peter Gimbel's camera jammed for the umpteenth time. The poor guy, he was so upset by it and I don't blame him. Jamming magazines are causing a lot of trouble. However, five rolls of good action came through okay.

We still have the whale and all systems are go for a night dive.

Tuesday, 5 June 1969

At last I have the energy to write again. It was a long night and even longer day. We entered the water about 12:39 A.M.., Peter Gimbel first, then myself; Stan and Ron came later. The water felt cool and refreshing. It revived me and I felt less tired. As the bubbles cleared, I lowered the cage a few feet and took my first good look. It was our privilege to gaze upon a scene of death and life, more horrible, more primeval than any I had seen before. We had entered a bygone age. No time machine could have done it better. The carnage around us had not changed, nor did it look different to how it had been and looked a million years ago.

The whale's mutilated body streamed blood and guts into the current. Huge sharks, fifty, one thousand, I couldn't count them, swirled in a frenzy around the carcass.

Where had they come from, these savage survivors from a bygone age? What ocean depths had hidden them from view during the day only to spew them forth in the darkness of night? I couldn't even guess.

Pale against the black water, they swam with their mouths agape, some carrying great hunks of torn flesh, gulping and swallowing without missing a beat of their powerful tails. One, larger than the rest, moved through the pack, cutting a path between his lesser fellows. He hit the whale with tremendous force, shuddering his way into the torn belly until only his vibrating tail and anal fins showed. Blood flowed like a green mist, obliterating the writhing body.

Stewart's lights hung like giant suspended stars, some 20 feet below our cage. Moving with the surge, their beams swung back and forth revealing, then losing, countless graceful bodies. One even larger shark could be seen moving in and out along the perimeter of illumination. I strained my eyes in its direction. Could it be the longed-for great white?

Something about the bobbing brilliance suddenly attracted this shark. It moved up from the fluttering darkness without haste, completely sure of its place. Peter and I watched in awe as this giant among giants carefully took the lights in its tremendous jaw, obliterating their brightness and plunging our world into darkness. Time and time again it mouthed the lights, feeling with its teeth the steel casing surrounding them. Curiosity suddenly satisfied, this great monster with the night black eyes and pale striped body passed our cage and circled several times before disappearing into the blackness. We didn't see the tiger shark again.

It was at least 15 feet and possibly 17 feet long. Its head looked to be the width of our cage. It was, next to the harmless whale shark, the largest I had ever seen.

By now Ron and Stan were entering their cage – ghostly shadows in a web of buckling steel. It was a relief to be able to descend fully. The heavy surface swell created a pitching motion that was becoming most unkind to my middle region. Almost immediately our troubles started.

Our light, which had been pulled over to us, proved extremely difficult to handle. The cage's tethering rope seemed longer than the power cable and it took all my strength to keep hold of the thing. We were tied to the *Terrier* which didn't help matters much. Her rise and fall in the heavy swell was many times that of the whale. Peter, realizing my difficulty, helped me pull a length of cable into the cage. He then hooked it around the valve on the spare air cylinder. This put tremendous strain on the valve, but we did manage to light and shoot several scenes before the strain became so great that it endangered the cage.

It then became another battle to extract the cable. We finally lost our light altogether when, in spite of our combined efforts, it pulled completely away from the cage, all but dragging us out of the open door.

Ron and Stan were having even greater problems. Their light cable had almost immediately become entangled around the whale. From there, it was twisted around the buoyancy tanks on our cage. They, like us, had been unable to hold their light after the first minute or so.

Unknown to us they were having even greater dramas on board the *Terrier*. Stewart Cody, seeing our problem, had leaped into a zodiac, cut the cages from the *Terrier*, and, with exceptional thought and courage, proceeded to untangle the twisted mess.

The milling sharks were a constant hindrance. Fortunately, we in the cage didn't realize our predicament. I wondered why we were unable to see the whale any more and why the light was fading and why the steady, familiar beat of the ship's engines had vanished, never realizing our cages were no longer tethered to anything but adrift at night surrounded by feeding sharks under the Indian Ocean. Not a comforting thought when one thinks about it. However, what one doesn't know doesn't hurt.

Somehow, Stewart sorted out the incredible mess, tethered us back to the whale, and eventually returned our lights to us. Peter, with his usual presence of mind, jammed our cable in the cage door. This gave me better freedom of movement and I could hold the light much steadier. The light was so heavy and awkward and I needed both hands to keep it under control and to point it in the general direction Peter was filming. Even more difficult was to manoeuvre the lights into the correct position and hold them there. Mostly, I judged my direction by watching the side of the camera housing and endeavouring to keep my light coordinated with this.

It was during one of our more difficult moments that a 10-foot oceanic whitetip chose to entangle itself in the connections at the top of our cage. An exciting few moments followed as we were buffeted from side to side. Terrified by the unaccustomed restrictions, the shark struggled frantically until finally it thrashed its way free. Peter gave me a look that said 'What's next?' What came next was something completely unplanned.

Somehow, during the confusion, both cages had drifted close into the whale. Ribbons of mutilated intestine streamed through the cages as they clanged together right where the sharks had ripped open the whale's belly. Ron was struggling frantically to keep his cage free of the jawbone. I could hardly see him for blood and gore which turned the surrounding water into a sort of raw soup. Although I knew it was impossible, I felt I was smelling, breathing, and tasting the stuff. I don't know how we eventually left the whale, perhaps the surface crew towed us away, but it was so pleasant to be away from that torn smelly hulk, I almost felt happy.

Peter showed me his pressure gauge. It read 0. I still had 900 pounds left but that didn't help Peter much. Stan signalled from the other cage that his air was low also. Both he and Ron had shot a 400-

foot roll of film. The zodiac picked them up first. As they left the water, the sharks, as though signalled, attacked the whale with, if possible, renewed fury. There is no doubt that they are far more active at night. Our cage, by now, was well away from the whale. In the darkness, I could hear the ship's engines coming closer. Suddenly, without warning, a tremendous shock vibrated the cage. We had drifted into the *Terrier*'s hull. God, do those cages take a hiding when alongside a rolling ship.

Peter handed out his camera and, although out of air, came down and made his 'after you' sign. This, I felt, was extremely thoughtful, because if there is any difficulty in my getting through the top hatch, he is always on hand to give me a good push in the rear. This night, however, I didn't want to go. The zodiac was in an impossible position for me to reach and I hung grimly to the cage as it ground into the ship's hull. Eventually someone leaned down and dragged me back on deck, an exhausted, trembling wreck.

I heard how the cages had nearly been lost when cut adrift from the *Terrier*. Stewart's quick thinking had saved us. He had the captain manoeuvre the vessel into a position down current to pick us up. Without this fast manoeuvre we could possibly still be going.

I managed to snatch three hours' sleep. More than Peter and Stan had, I would say. Peter had obtained permission from the Durban-based whaling company to keep the whale for another twelve hours.

We were up at daybreak. For once, the weather was really with us. Nothing could have been kinder than the oily swell and clear skies. We were in the water by 8:30 A.M. The sharks were still there, all of them. By now, dozens of albatrosses had gathered on the scene, their round white chests and ungainly web feet making a comical contrast to the fat sleek sharks in our underwater world. I tried to touch an albatross on the foot, but he bent down and gave me such a nip I forgot the idea immediately. Ron, I noticed, tried the same thing and was nipped also. Almost as bad as the sharks, those birds; just as well they are not underwater swimmers.

We were now working completely out of the cages. Sharks bumped and jostled around us. Many were 10 to 12 feet in length and very fat. The blue sharks were even longer and by far the most beautiful with their slender blue bodies and big black eyes. I was feeling very tired but pushed and poked sharks to the best of my ability. Also, my right arm was beginning to ache from the constant jarring as I hit the sharks. An old skiing injury to the elbow didn't help much either.

Ron was testing the powerheads. We needed to know that they would work properly if there was an emergency. He hit several sharks without much result. The powerheads we have on this trip use a weaker cartridge than the ones we use in Australia. None of the sharks appeared to die. In fact they all kept swimming and feeding in fine style. Then Ron tried something else. Something he had often wondered about. Would it be possible to kill one with a knife?

I guess it's a question that all divers would like to know the answer to. Using the ship's grinder, Ron had a hollow razor-sharp double edge on his diver's knife. An 8- to 9-foot whitetip swam directly over Ron's head. Ron plunged in his knife up to the hilt. It slid down the throat between the pectoral fins and laid open the belly. His victim swam down into the vast blue nothing beneath us, leaving a trail of smoky green blood in its wake. Encouraged, Ron experimented further, having a stab at every shark unfortunate enough to swim within his reach. He soon discovered that even his super sharp knife would not penetrate the top of the shark's head at all or the back or any part other than the soft underbelly.

Around lunchtime, I went down in the cage with Peter Lake. Unknown to me the tethering rope attaching us to the whale had chafed through and we did a dazzling descent to around 80 feet before I realized we had a problem. I pulled down the air holder to stop our descent but nothing happened. The cylinder had exhausted its air supply. I became very frightened. There was a frantic turning on of air and switching around of dials which, thank heaven, caused us to rocket ahead of a massive stream of bubbles back to the surface. Peter Lake and I drifted along for a while, then someone noticed us and came in a zodiac to tow us back to the whale. What did my diving companion think of all this? Why, he simply thought I was giving him a bit of fun; he wasn't alarmed at any time though he did wonder why we went so deep. A perfect example of what you don't know doesn't worry you!

It was around 3:30 P.M. when we had our last and most spectacular dive. I arrived rather late on the scene, having had to change tanks after my dive with Peter Lake. Also, I took time off for rest and a coffee break. The whale was little more than a heap of torn, stinking flesh. The sharks, somehow sensing that soon the end would come, seemed to be making the most of what time was left. If possible, they attacked the whale with even greater vigour.

As I swam down, an incredible sight greeted my eyes. Peter Gimbel had, perhaps because it was the last chance, chosen now as the time to film his much-deserved close-ups of the sharks' teeth tearing into the whale. He was swimming up through the clouds of blood protected by Stan, who was fighting a terrific battle with his exhausted powerhead. Further down, Ron was sitting on top of a cage running off the last of his film. I moved in to help Stan, my weariness forgotten in the excitement. It looked like a suicide mission. Dozens of feeding sharks milled around us, diving into the whale, then swimming out again, huge lumps of oily flesh hanging from their maws, blood flowing from their gills.

Some hung to the carcass, shuddering their way through flesh and sinew, tearing, gulping, swallowing in a continuous spasm of gluttony. Peter was filming about three or four feet from the heads of a group of feeding sharks. I whacked, hit and thumped as hard and as fast as I could. A quick glance at Stan showed him to be doing the same. We formed a triangle with Peter facing the whale, Stan and myself facing outwards. A shark banged me so hard on the shoulder I nearly dropped my powerhead. Peter filmed away calmly as though the sharks were toothless minnows, carefully lining up his shots to get the best action.

Another shark about 7 feet in length bumped me gently in the side. The first I knew of it was when it hit me. He actually mouthed my waist and a terrible tingle went over my body, but he apparently decided I was not what he wanted and moved on into the whale. At one stage, I rubbed against a feeding shark. Its vibrating body next to mine felt terrible, like some primitive shuddering monster in a nightmare. It was, I think, my only moment of fear during the entire time I was diving out from Durban in the Indian Ocean. Even then, I think it was less fear than revulsion.

Suddenly, for a moment, I realized how close I was to the bait, what was going on around me and how out of place I was. Peter Gimbel seemed to like it up there in the gore and blood, he took so darn long getting those last few close-ups.

Finally, he gave his little 'film's out' sign. I took one last look. Sharks, hundreds of them, milled in the vicinity of the whale. Out and down as far as we could see their ominous shapes glided silently to and fro, already gorged to the hilt, but reluctant to leave the banquet. Ron swam up to join us. We entered the cages and ascended. Our trip back in time was over.

We re-entered our present-day world, tired, hungry, cold, but elated. No one else in the world had done what we had done. Without the film, it would have been unbelievable. While unsuiting on board, Ron told a horrifying story. During the time Peter, Stan, and I were up with the whale, Ron was filming from the top of his cage when a large shark rammed him on the side of his head with its nose. The blow was so hard Ron went dizzy, saw stars, and fought to regain consciousness. Had he blacked out completely, he would have fallen off the cage and sunk into the depths without any of us being aware of what had happened. The water here is 2 miles deep. I would never have seen Ron again.

My arm ached from hitting sharks – in fact everything ached. It was a relief to get rid of the scuba tanks. Stan came up with a good theory as to why we were still alive. He reasoned, and very well, too, that the sharks, after realizing we were not easy prey although still curious, came to accept us just as some more marine creatures that had come to the feast. There were albatross, rainbow runners, kingfish, and three species of shark, so why not humans? Certainly, there was enough whale for everyone.

I crashed into bed, an exhausted mess, immediately following dinner – only sleep eluded me. Every time I closed my eyes and even when they were open, all I could see were sharks swimming towards me, around me, nuzzling me and, in my mind, I wearily beat them off. At 9:30, I was still, in my mind, fighting a thousand sharks. They plagued me, gave me no rest. Ron was tossing around, too, as though he had a shark in bed with him. I called 'What are you doing?' and he said, 'Fighting sharks.' We both took tranquilizers and finally slept.

3
From *Jaws*

Peter Benchley

Peter Benchley's best seller *Jaws* needs little introduction. The excerpt chosen takes place shortly after the shark hunt begins. Anyone who has ever sat in a dirty little fishing boat, surrounded by burley, waiting for a shark could not help but be touched by the truth and power of Benchley's descriptions.

Reading it, I heard the sounds and smelled the smells, for this segment is true to life. It really is like this. He describes to perfection a situation that Ron and I have experienced many times.

The shark is there and the waiting men know it, but they are powerless. They must wait on the shark; he, not they, controls the situation.

Be it the first time or the thirtieth, it is always the same when you see the great white shark approaching the cage. Hooper staring enthralled, impelled to flee but unable to move, captures the feeling perfectly.

I am amazed how clearly Benchley has reproduced my exact feelings and given them to a fictitious man in a fictitious situation. Of course, our sharks have always been repelled by the cage within which we work. Even the largest of them dislikes the feel of metal against teeth.

Benchley makes his fish completely believable, then gives it a brain which can think to plan the destruction of three men. No wonder that this shark inflamed the imagination of so many people, causing the beaches to be deserted and thousands of sharks to be slaughtered in a frenzy of mass hatred.

The general public believed all sharks could think and act according to a plan and they became afraid. I believe that this is part of the key to the success of *Jaws* and the fascination it has for the general public.

■

At eleven-thirty, Brody was startled by a sharp resonant *snap*. Quint leaped down the ladder, across the deck, and on to the transom. He picked up the harpoon and held it at his shoulder, scanning the water around the stern.

'What the hell was that?' said Brody.

'He's back.'

'How do you know? What was that noise?'

'Twine snapping. He took one of the squid.'

'Why would it snap? Why wouldn't he chew right through it?'

'He probably never bit down on it. He sucked it in, and the twine came tight behind his teeth when he closed his mouth. He went like this, I imagine' – Quint jerked his head to the side – 'and the line parted.'

'How could we hear it snap if it snapped under water?'

'It didn't snap under water, for Christ sake! It snapped right there.' Quint pointed to a few inches of limp twine hanging from a cleat amidships.

'Oh,' said Brody. As he looked at the remnant, he saw another piece of twine – a few feet farther up the gunwale – go limp. 'There's another one,' he said. He stood and walked to the gunwale and pulled in the line. 'He must be right underneath us.'

Quint said, 'Anybody care to go swimming?'

'Let's put the cage overboard,' said Hooper.

'You're kidding,' said Brody.

'No, I'm not. It might bring him out.'

'With you in it?'

'Not at first. Let's see what he does. What do you say, Quint?'

'Might as well,' said Quint. 'Can't hurt just to put it in the water, and you paid for it.' He put down the harpoon, and he and Hooper walked to the cage.

They tipped the cage on its side, and Hooper opened the top hatch and crawled through it. He removed the scuba tank, regulator, face mask, and neoprene wet suit, and set them on the deck. They tipped the cage upright again and slid it across the deck to the starboard gunwale. 'You got a couple of lines?' said Hooper. 'I want to make it fast to the boat.' Quint went below and returned with two coils of rope. They tied one to an after cleat, one to a cleat amidships, then secured the ends to the bars on top of the cage. 'Okay,' said Hooper. 'Let's push her over.' They lifted the cage, tipped it backwards, and pushed it overboard. It sank until the ropes stopped it, a few feet beneath the surface. There it rested, rising and falling slowly in the swells. The three men stood at the gunwale, looking into the water.

'What makes you think this'll bring him up?' said Brody.

'I didn't say "up",' said Hooper, 'I said "out". I think he'll come out and have a look at it, to see whether he wants to eat it.'

'That won't do us any damn good,' said Quint. 'I can't stick him if he's twelve feet under water.'

'Once he comes out,' said Hooper, 'maybe he'll come up. We're not having any luck with anything else.'

But the fish did not come out. The cage lay quietly in the water, unmolested.

'There goes another squid,' said Quint, pointing forward. 'He's there, all right.' He leaned overboard and shouted, 'God damn you, fish! Come out where I can have a shot at you.'

After fifteen minutes, Hooper said, 'Oh well,' and went below. He reappeared moments later, carrying a movie camera in a waterproof housing, and what looked to Brody like a walking stick with a thong on one end.

'What are you doing?' Brody said.

'I'm going down there. Maybe that'll bring him out.'

'You're out of your goddamn mind. What are you going to do if he does come out?'

'First, I'm going to take some pictures of him. Then I'm going to try to kill him.'

'With what, may I ask?'

'This.' Hooper held up the stick.

'Good thinking,' Quint said with a derisive cackle. 'If that doesn't work you can tickle him to death.'

'What is that?' said Brody.

'Some people call it a bang stick. Others call it a powerhead. Anyway, it's basically an underwater gun.' He pulled both ends of the stick, and it came apart in two pieces. 'In here,' he said, pointing to a chamber at the point where the stick had come apart, 'you put a twelve-gauge shotgun shell.' He took a shotgun shell from his pocket and pushed it into the chamber, then rejoined the two ends of the stick. 'Then, when you get close enough to the fish, you jab it at him and the shell goes off. If you hit him right – in the brain's the only sure place – you kill him.'

'Even a fish that big?'

'I think so. If I hit him right.'

'And if you don't? Suppose you miss by just a hair.'

'That's what I'm afraid of.'

'I would be, too,' said Quint. 'I don't think I'd like five thousand pounds of pissed-off dinosaur trying to eat me.'

'That's not my worry,' said Hooper. 'What concerns me is that if I miss, I might drive him off. He'd probably sound, and we'd never know if he died or not.'

'Until he ate someone else,' said Brody.

'That's right.'

'You're fucking crazy,' said Quint.

'Am I, Quint? You're not having much success with this fish. We could stay here all month and let him eat your bait right out from under us.'

'He'll come up,' said Quint. 'Mark my words.'

'You'll be dead of old age before he comes up, Quint. I think this fish has you all shook. He's not playing by the rules.'

Quint looked at Hooper and said evenly, 'You telling me my business, boy?'

'No. But I am telling you I think this fish is more than you can handle.'

'That's right, boy? You think you can do better'n Quint?'

'Call it that if you want. I think I can kill the fish.'

'Fine and dandy. You're gonna get your chance.'

Brody said, 'Come on. We can't let him go in that thing.'

'What are *you* bitchin' about?' said Quint. 'From what I seen, you just as soon he went down there and never come up. At least that'd stop him from –'

'Shut your mouth!' Brody's emotions were jumbled. Part of him didn't care whether Hooper lived or died – might even relish the prospect of Hooper's death. But such vengeance would be hollow – and quite possibly, unmerited. Could he really wish a man dead? No. Not yet.

'Go on,' Quint said to Hooper. 'Get in that thing.'

'Right away.' Hooper removed his shirt, sneakers, and trousers, and began to pull the neoprene suit over his legs. 'When I'm inside,' he said, forcing his arms into the rubber sleeves of the jacket, 'stand up here and keep an eye. Maybe you can use the rifle if he gets close enough to the surface.' He looked at Quint. 'You can be ready with the harpoon . . . if you want to.'

'I'll do what I'll do,' said Quint. 'You worry about yourself.'

When he was dressed, Hooper fitted the regulator on to the neck of the air tank, tightened the wingnut that held it in place, and opened the air valve. He sucked two breaths from the tank to make sure it was feeding air. 'Help me put this on, will you?' he said to Brody.

Brody lifted the tank and held it while Hooper slipped his arms through the straps and fastened a third strap around his middle. He put the face mask on his head. 'I should have brought weights,' said Hooper.

Quint said, 'You should have brought brains.'

Hooper put his right wrist through the thong at the end of the powerhead, picked up the camera with his right hand, and said, 'Okay.' He walked to the gunwale. 'If you'll each take a rope and pull, that'll bring the cage to the surface. Then I'll open the hatch and go in through the top, and you can let the ropes go. It'll hang by the ropes. I won't use the flotation tanks unless one of the ropes breaks.'

'Or gets chewed through,' said Quint.

Hooper looked at Quint and smiled. 'Thanks for the thought.'

Quint and Brody pulled on the ropes, and the cage rose in the water. When the hatch broke the surface, Hooper said, 'Okay, right there.' He spat in the face mask, rubbed the saliva around on the glass, and fitted the mask over his face. He reached for the regulator tube, put the mouthpiece in his mouth, and took a breath. Then he bent over the gunwale, unlatched the top of the hatch and flipped it open. He started to pull a knee on the gunwale, but stopped. He took the mouthpiece out of his mouth and said, 'I forgot something.' His nose was enclosed in the mask so his voice sounded thick and nasal. He walked across the deck and picked up his trousers. He rummaged through the pockets until he found what he was looking for. He unzipped his wet-suit jacket.

'What's that?' said Brody.

Hooper held up a shark's tooth, rimmed in silver. It was a duplicate of the one he had given to Ellen. He dropped it inside his wetsuit and zipped up the jacket. 'Can't be too careful,' he said, smiling. He crossed the deck again, put his mouthpiece in his mouth, and kneeled on the gunwale. He took a final breath and dived overboard through the open hatch. Brody watched him go, wondering if he really wanted to know the truth about Hooper and Ellen.

Hooper stopped himself before he hit the bottom of the cage. He curled around and stood up. He reached out to the top of the hatch and pulled it closed. Then he looked up at Brody, put the thumb and index finger of his left hand together in the okay sign, and ducked down.

'I guess we can let go,' said Brody. They released the ropes and let the cage descend until the hatch was about four feet beneath the surface.

'Get the rifle,' said Quint. 'It's on the rack below. It's all loaded.' He climbed on to the transom and lifted the harpoon to his shoulder.

Brody went below, found the rifle, and hurried back on deck. He opened the breach and slid a cartridge into the chamber. 'How much air does he have?' he said.

'I don't know,' said Quint. 'However much he has, I doubt he'll live to breathe it.'

'Maybe you're right. But you said yourself you never know what these fish will do.'

'Yeah, but this is different. This is like putting your hands in a fire and hoping you won't get burned. A sensible man don't *do* it.'

Below, Hooper waited until the bubbly froth of his descent had dissipated. There was water in his mask, so he tilted his head backwards, pressed on the top of the faceplate, and blew through his nose until the mask was clear. He felt serene. It was the pervasive sense of freedom and ease that he always felt when he dived. He was alone in blue silence speckled with shafts of sunlight that danced through the water. The only sounds were those he made breathing – a deep, hollow noise as he breathed in, a soft thudding of bubbles as he exhaled. He held his breath, and the silence was complete. Without weights, he was too buoyant, and he had to hold on to the bars to keep his tank from clanging against the hatch overhead. He turned around and looked up at the hull of the boat, a grey body that sat above him, bouncing slowly. At first, the cage annoyed him. It confined him, restricted him, prevented from enjoying the grace of underwater movement. But then he remembered why he was there, and he was grateful.

He looked for the fish. He knew it couldn't be sitting beneath the boat, as Quint had thought. It could not 'sit' anywhere, could not rest or stay still. It had to move to survive.

Even with the bright sunlight, the visibility in the murky water was poor – no more than forty feet. Hooper turned slowly around, trying to pierce the edge of gloom and grasp any sliver of colour or movement. He looked beneath the boat, where the water turned from blue to grey to black. Nothing. He looked at his watch, calculating that if he controlled his breathing, he could stay down for at least half an hour more.

Carried by the tide, one of the small white squid slipped between the bars of the cage and, tethered by twine, fluttered in Hooper's face. He pushed it out of the cage.

He glanced downwards, started to look away, then snapped his eyes down again. Rising at him from the darkling blue – slowly, smoothly – was the shark. It rose with no apparent effort, an angel of death gliding towards an appointment foreordained.

Hooper stared, enthralled, impelled to flee but unable to move. As the fish drew nearer, he marvelled at its colours: the flat brown-greys seen on the surface had vanished. The top of the immense body was a hard ferrous grey, bluish where dappled with streaks of sun. Beneath the lateral line, all was creamy, ghostly, white.

Hooper wanted to raise his camera, but his arm would not obey. In a minute, he said to himself, in a minute.

The fish came closer, silent as a shadow, and Hooper drew back. The head was only a few feet from the cage when the fish turned and began to pass before Hooper's eyes – casually, as if in proud display of its incalculable mass and power. The snout passed first, then the jaw, slack and smiling, armed with row upon row of serrate triangles. And then the black, fathomless eye seemingly riveted upon him. The gills rippled – bloodless wounds in the steely skin.

Tentatively, Hooper stuck a hand through the bars and touched the flank. It felt cold and hard, not clammy but smooth as vinyl. He let his finger tips caress the flesh – past the pectoral fins, the pelvic fin, the thick, firm genital claspers – until finally (the fish seemed to have no end) they were slapped away by the sweeping tail.

The fish continued to move away from the cage. Hooper heard

faint popping noises, and he saw three straight spirals of angry bubbles speed from the surface, then slow and stop, well above the fish. Bullets. Not yet, he told himself. One more pass for pictures. The fish began to turn, banking, the rubbery pectoral fins changing pitch.

'What the hell is he doing down there?' said Brody. 'Why didn't he jab him with the gun?'

Quint didn't answer. He stood on the transom, harpoon clutched in his fist, peering into the water. 'Come up, fish,' he said. 'Come to Quint.'

'Do you see it?' said Brody. 'What's it doing?'

'Nothing. Not yet anyway.'

The fish had moved off to the limit of Hooper's vision – a spectral silver-grey blur tracing a slow circle. Hooper raised his camera and pressed the trigger. He knew the film would be worthless unless the fish moved in once more, but he wanted to catch the beast as it emerged from the darkness.

Through the viewfinder he saw the fish turn towards him. It moved fast, tail thrusting vigorously, mouth opening and closing as if gasping for breath. Hooper raised his right hand to change the focus. Remember to change it again, he told himself, when it turns.

But the fish did not turn. A shiver travelled the length of its body as it closed in on the cage. It struck the cage head on, the snout ramming between two bars and spreading them. The snout hit Hooper in the chest and knocked him backwards. The camera flew from his hands, and the mouthpiece shot from his mouth. The fish turned on its side, and the pounding tail forced the great body farther into the cage. Hooper groped for his mouthpiece but couldn't find it. His chest was convulsed with the need for air.

'It's attacking!' screamed Brody. He grabbed one of the tether ropes and pulled, desperately trying to raise the cage.

'God damn your fucking soul!' Quint shouted.

'Throw it! Throw it!'

'I can't throw it! I gotta get him on the surface! Come up, you devil! You prick!'

The fish slid backwards out of the cage and turned sharply to the right in a tight circle. Hooper reached behind his head, found the regulator tube, and followed it with his hand until he located the mouthpiece. He put it in his mouth and, forgetting to exhale first, sucked for air. He got water, and he gagged and choked until at last the mouthpiece cleared and he drew an agonized breath. It was then he saw the wide gap in the bars and saw the giant head lunging through it. He raised his hands above his head, grasping at the escape hatch.

The fish rammed through the space between the bars, spreading them still farther with each thrust of its tail, Hooper, flattened against the back of the cage, saw the mouth reaching, straining for him. He remembered the power head, and he tried to lower his right arm and grab it. The fish thrust again, and Hooper saw with the terror of doom that the mouth was going to reach him.

The jaws closed around his torso. Hooper felt a terrible pressure as if his guts were compacted. He jabbed his fist into the black eye. The fish bit down, and the last thing Hooper saw before he died was the eye gazing at him through a cloud of his own blood.

'He's got him!' cried Brody. 'Do something!'

'The man is dead,' Quint said.

'How do you know? We may be able to save him.'

'He is dead.'

Holding Hooper in its mouth, the fish backed out of the cage, sank a few feet, clawing, swallowing the viscera that were squeezed into its gullet. Then it shuddered and thrust forward with its tail, driving itself and prey upward in the water.

'He's coming up!' said Brody.

'Grab the rifle!' Quint cocked his hand for the throw.

The fish broke water fifteen feet from the boat, surging upward in a shower of spray. Hooper's body protruded from each side of the mouth, head and arms hanging limply down one side, knees, calves, and feet from the other.

In the few seconds while the fish was clear of the water, Brody thought he saw Hooper's glazed eyes staring open through his face mask. As if in contempt and triumph, the fish suspended for an instant, challenging mortal vengeance.

Simultaneously, Brody reached for the rifle and Quint cast the harpoon. The target was huge, a field of white belly, and the distance was not too great for a successful throw above water. But as Quint threw, the fish began to slide down in the water, and the iron went high.

For another instant, the fish remained on the surface, its head out of water. Hooper hanging from its mouth.

'Shoot!' Quint yelled. 'For Christ sake, shoot!'

Brody shot without aiming. The first two shots hit the water in front of the fish. The third, to Brody's horror, struck Hooper in the neck.

'Here, give me the goddam thing!' said Quint, grabbing the rifle from Brody. In a single, quick motion he raised the rifle to his shoulder and squeezed off two shots. But the fish, with a last, vacant gaze, had already begun to slip beneath the surface. The bullets plopped harmlessly into the swirl where the head had been.

The fish might never have been there. There was no noise, save the whisper of a breeze. From the surface the cage seemed undamaged. The water was calm. The only difference was that Hooper was gone.

'What do we do now?' said Brody. 'What in the name of God can we do now? There's nothing left. We might as well go back.'

'We'll go back,' said Quint. 'For now.'

'For now? What do you mean? There's nothing we can do. The fish is too much for us. It's not real, not natural.'

'Are you beaten, man?'

'I'm beaten. All we can do is wait until God or nature or whatever the hell is doing this to us decides we've had enough. It's out of man's hands.'

'Not mine,' said Quint. 'I am going to kill that thing.'

'I'm not sure I can get any more money after what happened today.'

'Keep your money. This is no longer a matter of money.'

'What do you mean?' Brody looked at Quint, who was standing on the stern, looking at the spot where the fish had been, as if he expected it to reappear at any moment clutching the shredded corpse in its mouth. He searched the sea, craving another confrontation.

Quint said to Brody, 'I am going to kill that fish. Come if you want. Stay home if you want. But I am going to kill that fish.'

As Quint spoke, Brody looked into his eyes. They seemed as dark and bottomless as the eye of the fish. 'I'll come,' said Brody. 'I don't guess I have any choice.'

'No,' said Quint. 'We have no choice.' He took his knife from its sheath and handed it to Brody. 'Here. Cut that cage loose and let's get out of here.'

4

The Filming for *Jaws*

Valerie Taylor

This story is taken straight from my diary. It differs considerably from the picture that Carl Gottlieb paints in *The Jaws Log*. He was at a disadvantage, having to rely on information acquired long after we had finished the live shark shooting.

I wrote every day, sometimes twice a day, about what actually happened. This story is not complete. I stuck to the main points, leaving out the small everyday happenings. It tells without alteration or glamorization how we went about filming the great white shark and how some of the difficult scenes of the sharks attacking the cage were obtained.

When we were shooting the live shark footage, none of us had any idea that the film would be such a tremendous success. To Ron and me it was just another filming job, our eighth at that time, involving great white sharks.

It was the first time that Ron had to work to a script. Fortunately it was not the final script, so there was some leeway with the action.

For editing purposes, a series of shots showing the shark swimming towards and away from the camera was required. Cage bars were not to be shown. This meant that to film these sequences, Ron had to work out of the cage.

Working outside of the cage is not as dangerous as it sounds. Ron always stays next to the door, so, if need be, he can slip inside in a few seconds. It becomes more dangerous when there are two or more sharks circling because only one can be watched at a time, but Ron believes taking the occasional risk to be part of his job, and he is always very careful.

Even so, during the *Jaws* filming, Ron miscalculated and actually pushed himself away from a shark by ramming his camera against its mouth. It was one of the two dangerous incidents that occurred. The other is described in detail here.

■

A ribbon of harsh granite boulders breaks the ocean's surface about 14 miles off the South Australian coast. Over a hundred years ago, explorer Captain Matthew Flinders first observed these bleak, spray-washed outcrops.

Flinders considered the area a hazard to future shipping and as a warning to all who dared venture forth upon the southern ocean, he named the place Dangerous Reef.

Today, this name means more than just a hazard to shipping. It is a warning to all. Inhabiting the cold, grey waters surrounding Dangerous Reef, *Carcharodon carcharias*, the great white shark, hunts his prey. An attacker of all who dare cross his path, this giant survivor from a bygone age has become to man the epitome of terror in the sea.

Since 1965, my husband, an underwater cameraman, has hunted the white shark with his camera, capturing on film the most dramatic and exciting scenes of shark behaviour ever recorded. Ron does not consider the shark an indiscriminate killer, but a poor dumb brute goaded by an unsatiable appetite into awe-inspiring eating feats.

The great white is nature's garbage man: efficient, inexpensive, and nonpolluting. His job is to keep the oceans free from large masses of garbage; be it a dead whale or a cardboard box, the great white devours all, leaving the oceans cleaner with his passing. Man, with all his knowledge, could never do the job as well.

Early in 1974, Ron and I started preparing to film white sharks once again. The Zanuck-Brown company planned to produce a film version of Peter Benchley's best-selling novel *Jaws* for Universal Studios.

Zanuck-Brown were going all out to make the shark a living, thinking star attraction. Ron was to shoot real whites in their natural element for intercutting with a man-made mechanical giant.

Smaller cages were especially constructed. A former American jockey, Carl Rizzo, was to be sent across as a stuntman and Carl was to double for the full-size actor, who would be working with the main production crew in the United States.

The villain of *Jaws* is a 26-foot white shark and this is not as outlandish as it sounds. The largest white shark ever seen was taken in South Australia, and supposedly measured over 36 feet. Twenty-foot great whites are uncommon, but still claimed to be seen off the South Australian coast.

Big-game fishermen have not landed any white sharks larger than 18 feet. They have been hooked over 20 feet in length, but a shark that size is so strong and heavy, the game fisherman would need a winch to land it. The shark portrayed so realistically by Mr Benchley in *Jaws* could easily be a true animal. There is certainly no proof to the contrary.

Ron and I arrived in Port Lincoln, South Australia, on 12 February 1974. Our good friend Rodney Fox had everything organized for the filming expedition. He had bought a sick horse from a farmer; it was slaughtered and the carcass prepared for use as shark baits. He had also ordered six bins of minced tuna heads, which we would use to try and burley in the shark.

The 35-foot *Trade Wind* had been chartered for several weeks, and Dick Leach was our skipper. We like working with Dick; he is cheerful, hard-talking, and a fine seaman.

The Americans arrived in Port Lincoln on the thirteenth. Jim Hogan, our production manager, had been rushed across as a replacement for his contemporary, Frank Arrigo, who had suffered an unexpected heart attack shortly after arriving in Sydney.

With Jim was little Carl Rizzo. At first I found Carl shy and hard to communicate with. He had been a good jockey and now trained racehorses. Sometimes he doubled for children on horseback in feature films, which was how he became a stuntman.

Carl had been sent to double under water for the main actors. He had never been scuba diving in the ocean – his entire experience consisted of a couple of brief lessons in an enclosed pool. Hollywood had sent him to us, this gentle little man, and we were supposed to bundle him into a cage, tie baits to the bars, lower the cage into the icy turbulent southern ocean and then wait for the sharks to attack. I guess that is the sort of stuff Hollywood lives on, but to us, who knew sharks and the oceans so well, it all seemed incredible.

On the sixteenth, we were finally ready to leave. There had been a holdup in the arrival of the American cages, which had delayed us two days. We left the Port Lincoln wharf by midday, Rodney leading the way in his 19-foot fibreglass abalone boat, *Skippy*. It was a pleasant trip to Dangerous Reef. The sun shone and a brisk southeasterly wind whipped the southern ocean into a living carpet of white and blue.

The lee at Dangerous Reef was hardly a lee at all. A sloppy swell was running as usual around the point and made the *Trade Wind* toss in an annoying fashion.

Dick anchored in 37 feet of water. The chum buckets were lowered and a dozen bloody baits strung in an appetizing fashion along the hull. It was an uncomfortable anchorage, but we had no choice and settled down to wait.

On the reef itself hundreds of Australian sea lions could be seen. Many had little dark brown babies, newly born. These sea lion pups are a favourite source of food for the white pointer. They are not born as swimmers and have to be taught by their mothers. During the learning-to-swim period, the little pups are extremely vulnerable. Nature's culler, the great white shark, patrols the breeding colonies, ever ready to strike down the weak, the slow, or the unwary.

Early on the seventeenth, our first white shark moved up the burley slick. Ron loaded his 35-mm Camaflex. The cage was rolled over the stern and Ron, sleek as a seal in his black wetsuit, climbed down onto the duckboard. The shark was a good one, 13 feet long and unafraid. He came straight in to feed. The script calls for him to be scarred around the nose, so while he was busy chewing the prop, Rodney, using my lipstick, reached down and painted on a few scars. Ron shot 400 feet of film, then changed cameras.

Next, I went down in the cage, dressed like the scientist in the film, and Ron did a roll of over-the-shoulder shots. The rough surface conditions made everything very difficult. By the time my tank had run dry, I was bitterly cold and rather battered. It was hard work in the cage. The surge tossed it around in a most aggravating fashion, making it impossible for steady photography. Around midafternoon, the shark became bored with us and left.

The following day was marred by a steady drizzle. However, to everyone's great joy, a new shark came in and we began to tease him with the baits. Ron immediately went down in the cage. The shark action was not good, but at least it stayed around, swimming in a slow smooth pattern, back and forth, back and forth.

The *Trade Wind* pitched like a mad thing; the wind blew like ice from the South Pole. My nose told me the baits were beginning to ripen rather well. Only the shark seemed unaffected by the weather and the rolling boat. Ron decided he wanted Carl down in his smaller cage. Getting Carl ready was difficult. He was not used to the movement of the boat. It was Rodney's job to get Carl in and out of his cage, which, for the purpose of the film, was attached to the abalone winch on Rod's boat. I felt from the start that Carl, a rank beginner, could never handle the rough conditions, but he was being paid to try and try he did.

Dick and Rodney lowered Carl into the small cage, but no sooner had he disappeared under the surface, they had to pull him back because water had entered his mouthpiece. Three times Carl tried to go down in his cage, without success. The water was too rough for a beginner. Finally Ron abandoned the idea – he would have to wait for calmer conditions.

One week and not much luck later, on 26 February, we were anchored again, in the same position. The sea lions watched our arrival with the look of someone who had seen it all before. Weather conditions were still not good at Dangerous Reef, but at least it was sunny.

While the men were eating lunch, I wandered out onto the deck and started throwing minced tuna into the water. After about ten minutes, a 13-foot shark appeared just under the surface and started cutting to and fro through the burley. I called, 'Shark,' and threw some blood in his path.

Rodney leaped up from the table, followed by everyone else, but in his great hurry to see the shark, his finger somehow became jammed behind the cabin's narrow sliding door. No one could squeeze past, and Rodney could not free his finger. I looked back to see Rodney blocking the door with his body and yelling a few choice words. I thought some great catastrophe was about to happen, but at that moment Rod's finger came free and the men spilled out onto the deck.

Everyone immediately leaped into action, lunch forgotten. Here is what I wrote in my diary at the time:

'The big shark liked blood. He moved closer. Tasting the water. More minced tuna was thrown in and Ron's cage lowered. Carl's smaller but much heavier and stronger cage was manhandled into position next to Rodney's boat. It was held in place by a hand-operated abalone winch. Carl was suited up and helped into his cage. Conditions were calmer now than they had been for weeks. The shark seemed afraid of the divers. He was approaching no closer to the cages than 8 feet. From the deck we could see the brute circling around. It is terribly frustrating to be down in the cage watching and waiting, every nerve concentrating on the shark, wondering from what direction he will come, then having him pass swiftly as a swallow, too far away for decent photography. On the deck we can see the shark long before Ron. I tried to will him closer to the cages. I think we all did, but the beast paid no heed to our silent thoughts and kept his distance. He was tied to us by his instinct to feed, by our trails of blood and horsemeat baits, yet he hesitated in his approach until, finally, Ron, frustrated, surfaced and climbed back on board. Carl was also brought to the surface. He had managed very well, only the shark had performed poorly. Ron and Carl had been on deck a few minutes, when a new shark appeared. He came straight and strong and fearing nothing. This was the type of shark we had been waiting for. A shark who moved, thought, and behaved like the fish Peter Benchley had written about so convincingly in his book.

'Ron's cage bounced as the fish attacked the flotation tanks. Immediately Ron put on a fresh scuba tank, asking Carl to do the same.

'The shark circled closer. We could all see Ron, six feet down, sitting on top of his cage filming, a rather risky method he had been using for some time in an effort to get shots without bars in the foreground. I was frantic that he should take such a chance. By now, there were three sharks around. Ron couldn't look everywhere at once. He was gambling on the other sharks remaining cautious while he concentrated on filming the more aggressive newcomer. Several times, watching from the deck, we saw Ron push the shark in the mouth with his camera.

'I loaded a ·303 army bullet into the powerhead on my speargun and placed it within easy reach. Then I told Greg Dean, the assistant, if there was any trouble, I would jump in with the gun and that I expected him to help me in the water. Greg said, "Sure," and he meant it, too.

'Later Ron explained how his scuba harness had become hooked in the wire mesh, stopping him from moving inside the cage when the shark attacked. Not used to aggression, particularly in the form of a cold, hard camera housing, the white gave way and, no doubt, pondered this strange series of events before instinct forced him to try again.

'Eventually, Carl was ready to dive. Dick helped him into Rodney's 19-foot runabout, *Skippy*. Rodney was busy adjusting Carl's mouthpiece when our new shark swam around *Skippy*'s stern. The beast cut close to the hull, bumping the steel ropes attaching Carl's cage to the winch. Feeling the unfamiliar metal cable against his nose, the shark lunged blindly forward, pushing his great pointed snout further between the cable. Water flew. The *Skippy* rolled onto her side, dragged down by a half ton of fighting fish. A huge head rose above the spray twisting and turning, black maw gaping in a frenzy of rage and pain. Triangular teeth splintered as they tore the restricting metal. The brute dove, his cycle tail whipping the air six feet above the surface.

'Carl stood frozen with shock. As Rodney pulled him back, the tail brushed Carl's face. Had Rodney been two seconds slower, the little stuntman would have been killed, his head crushed into pulp.

'Suddenly, I awoke from my spellbound trance and ran for the movie camera. Greg Dean grabbed his still camera. We both started shooting. Jim, who was holding an inch and three quarter sisal rope attached to *Skippy* had the thing snap in his hand, throwing him off-balance back into the burley drum. How Jim held against a pull so hard it could break a new 1,000-pound breaking strain rope I don't know and neither does he, but many unusual things happened in that short space of time. Under the strain, the winch began to bend. The great white shark's body crashed into the hull. The noise was incredible, splitting wood, thrashing water, cage against boat, shark against boat.

'Again and again the fish tried to dive, mindless of the havoc above, striving only for freedom in the cold dark depth below. Water was slopping over the deck. The winch bent further. There was a loud cracking. Suddenly, the *Skippy* sprang upright, minus her winch and part of the decking.

'A last mighty splash, then shark, cage, winch, and deck vanished in a boiling, foaming swirl. Had Carl been in the cage, he too would have vanished with no possible chance of survival.

'The *Skippy* sat quietly like a wounded bird. We also were silent, for there seemed little to say.

'Underwater from his cage, Ron had filmed the whole thing, starting when the shark swam around the motors. At first, Ron thought Carl must be in the cage. It wasn't until the shark, still entangled with the cage and winch, spun twisting in agony toward the ocean floor that he realized Carl must be safe.

'The writhing mess was headed straight for Ron, who had a few moments of real fear before the whole lot ploughed into the bottom only feet away, stirring the sediment into a billowing mushroom of obliterating sand. Ron continued to film and captured the shark suddenly darting away from the turbulence. By a miracle, it had struggled free.

'Somehow Ron managed to retrieve the cage and winch, tying both onto his own cage, so all could be dragged back to the *Trade Wind*. He actually moved his cage along by putting his hand through the bars and pushing on the ocean floor. It was a slow and painful process. Two more sharks hovered like vultures, following Ron's every move. Whether just curious or waiting the chance to attack, Ron couldn't say, but they stayed close, forcing Ron to remain in the cage for twenty minutes until the whole lot was physically dragged aboard by the men.'

Jim Hogan was as pleased as anything with the action. We played about a bit more with the sharks until it became too dark for good photography.

I cooked a big dinner, which was rather a celebration, then we headed back to port.

Jim left the following day with the film. He wanted it processed in Sydney, then sent to Universal in Los Angeles, so the director, Steve Spielberg, could see what had been shot up to date.

On the afternoon of 5 March, we received word from Hollywood to try and shoot more shark footage. As the cages had been repaired and Rodney's boat was still seaworthy, the following morning we once again headed out.

As we left we heard a report on the radio news that the abalone divers were complaining publicly about us burleying in sharks. An abalone diver had been attacked and killed in South Australia by a great white shortly before, and this, understandably, made the other abalone divers very nervous. Frustrated by the bad weather and frightened by the recent shark attack, a small group of divers had, it seems, decided to blame us, at least in part, for their misfortunes.

We arrived at Dangerous Reef around midmorning. Four drums were evenly spaced in front of the area where we usually anchor. It appeared they had been set to catch sharks. One had a small, very dead bronze whaler still attached. The drums were only of 12-gallon capacity, far too light to seriously hold a white, but certainly capable of hooking one and hurting him enough to make him very annoyed. It was obvious that the abalone divers were out to give us trouble.

We received a radio message from Jim Hogan telling us to quietly pack and return to Port Lincoln. We dropped all our baits and headed back. Later, we read in the local paper that the abalone divers claimed to have scared us off and that, if we ever returned to film sharks, they would follow us around dropping baited hooks next to us, wherever we were trying to work.

On 5 April, exactly fifteen days later, we were anchored at Dangerous Reef once again. Rodney had spoken to the abalone divers, explaining what we were trying to do. Provided we killed the white sharks after we filmed them, they promised to leave us in peace. We had no alternative but to agree to this request.

Three days and no sharks. Ron was becoming worried that he would not have any sharks to film, so we decided to make an all-out effort. The burley flow was doubled, producing an incredible feeding frenzy among the small fish around the stern. Dick and Rodney fished constantly, dragging in one quivering trevally after the other.

Still no sharks came, so we waited, watching the slick for the telltale sign of a fin breaking the surface. It seemed that now we were paying for our good luck and good sharks with no luck at all.

On the morning 12 April, Ron was up before daybreak, searching the slate grey water. No black fin cut the swell, all our baits hung untouched. We had sent an invitation across the ocean, our feast was waiting, we as hosts were waiting, but the guests declined to attend. The last of the minced tuna heads floated away. We could not go to find the shark, he had to come to us and, if he refused, we could do nothing about it.

By midmorning, we started to pack up the gear. Rodney cut the baits loose. I watched them sink slowly to the ocean floor, surrounded by a thousand small fish. The big fish we wanted so badly had not come; there was nothing else to be done. We headed home across the sunlit sea. Pacific gulls cried their farewells. They had fed magnificently on our baits and were sad to see us leave. The sea-lions I love to watch played on. They cared nothing for us, our hopes, our failures.

There is a charisma about this cold lonely place, where the gentle sea-lions live out their joyous lives and 'The White Death' patrols the cold green depths.

5
Filming Tiger Sharks

Valerie Taylor

My experience with tiger sharks is limited to seven sightings, of which only three resulted in a closer association. They are the big predators of the tropical oceans, patrolling the coral reefs in much the same way a great white patrols the seal islands in colder waters. It is proven that they do occasionally attack humans and, according to reports, have on rare occasions eaten them. However, under normal circumstances they are gentle, well behaved fish with an amazing ability to learn.

Next to the grey nurse, tigers are my favourite sharks. Like the great white they have a presence that is awesome to behold, and like the great white they remain somewhat of a mystery. Pregnant female tigers have been caught on many occasions. They give birth to large numbers of live young – up to seventy or more pups have been removed from dead females. A favourite photo for the game fisherman is to stand next to his catch with the aborted young in a neat row beside her.

They eat almost anything. At Heron Island on the southern end of the Barrier Reef, silky sharks and tiger sharks act as garbage men for the kitchen refuse. Once a day the scraps are dumped. I have seen tiger sharks eating celery, pineapple, loaves of bread, beer cans, and once, half a watermelon which he must have liked because he returned for the leftovers and swallowed them down as well.

Tiger sharks make wonderful pets and appear to live well in big aquariums. When in captivity they continually nuzzle the walls as though searching for a way out. Their keepers usually love them dearly. Unlike most sharks, tigers quickly learn to accept food from their attendant's hand and some will raise their heads above water for a pat when the keeper is nearby.

I have never felt even slightly threatened by a tiger in the open ocean. Hammerheads also seem to be easy-going this way. It is the smaller faster predators who can become a nuisance.

This segment is about the last two tigers I have met, one a male the other a female. Writing this I feel regret that I shall never see them again. They were both special animals and my life is richer for having met them.

■

We were working on a New Zealand feature film called *The Silent One*. Our location was Aitutaki in the Cook Islands, an idyllic cluster of atolls surrounding a large lagoon. Aitutaki appeared the perfect place to work. A section of the lagoon between two islands was fenced off using weld mesh, and the marine animals appearing in the film lived in this area.

A turtle was the main actor, but several important scenes needed a big shark. Alan Walters, director of the Raratonga Marine Zoo, was employed to find a suitable specimen for us to work with. Ron and I rather fancied a tiger, they look impressive but appeared to be very even tempered. We stipulated that it must not be ill-treated or damaged and that when we had finished it must be released. Alan agreed; like us he loves tiger sharks, having kept one in his aquarium for about six months. Several weeks later Alan and our new actor arrived at the location. A magnificent three metre (10 foot) male tiger in superb condition. During his first night in the lagoon he devoured one and a half large tuna. This pleased us greatly. A feeding animal is a healthy one.

The lagoon area was very large. It contained a coral reef where the turtles hung around, a floating raft for the above water crew, a second coral area in shallow water and hundreds of fish, some there naturally and some because we put them there.

As expected our shark was easily handled, a diver or snorkeller could send him in any direction by putting their hand on his head and forcing it in one direction or another. At no time did the shark behave in an aggressive way towards any of the divers pushing it around. One scene called for a young boy to stand on the lagoon floor in five metres (15 feet) of water while the shark passed. The boy wore no equipment at all, just a waist cloth. When the shark wranglers had our tiger in position the actor would submerge and wait for the shark to pass. If the shark swam the wrong way he was simply herded back into position to try again. He took it all very calmly, in fact calmness was a feature of the shark's personality. There was never any show of temper or attempt to bite. He understood the situation. He was trapped, we had trapped him, he was not being harmed and he might as well swim where we wanted him to. It was for him the easiest thing to do until he could find a way to escape.

One Sunday, as no one was working, I took my still camera into the lagoon to photograph the shark for myself. It was a hot sunny day, but due to a big tide the water was rather dirty. I waited against the weld mesh over the deepest section of the lagoon. A sort of channel ran through this area cut by the ebb and flow of the tide. Perhaps sensing this channel led to the open ocean, a large sole was trying to force his body through the mesh. As the shark only appeared about once every 15 minutes, I amused myself by watching the sole. We had noticed before that Cook Island soles are very intelligent. He tried the holes in the mesh horizontally, vertically, corner to corner then every hole all the way to the surface, all without success. Poor little sole, he appeared very dejected by his failure and sank back to the sand where he lay nose into a gap – a prisoner staring at freedom through the bars. Feeling sorry for him I swam down and began scooping sand away from under the mesh. The sole, sensing what was happening, became quite active. Eventually I had a gap about three quarters of a metre long and ten centimetres in height. Almost before I had moved away the sole swam through into the main lagoon area. I surfaced just as the shark appeared. Swimming in his slow careful way he nosed along the steel mesh, like the sole, seeking escape. I sank down, took a picture and the shark passed. Suddenly, when almost out of sight, he swung back and glided straight down to my recent excavation. Six metres above I watched in utter amazement as the shark examined the gap then pushed his blunt flat nose into it. He pushed a little, realised he could not squeeze through then, using his fins, braced his body on the sand and tried to lift the mesh up. Three times he tried, exerting more effort with each heave. The mesh did not move, so he backed away and continued circling. As far as I know he never looked at the gap again. What I found so astounding was not that he saw a change in the fence and investigated it, but that he did so with such speed and accuracy. To my way of thinking he acted with commonsense and intelligence. When the filming was completed he was given the freedom he so desperately longed for when Alan released him into the open ocean.

My other tiger shark we met at Marion Reef in the Coral Sea. She was a female of rare physical beauty and charm who appeared from the deep while we were setting up a feeding frenzy for grey reef sharks. Her appearance was quite unexpected. Three metres (10 feet) of striped perfection. She must have picked up the smell of dead tuna from our bait box drifting down the pass. Her arrival caused a flurry of excitement. The big baits were in a box that was tied closed. I carried a small fish. The rest was in the dinghy. She was sniffing around the bait box but had no hope of getting in. I knew the best way to keep her interested would be to quickly give her something to eat, but the only available food was in my hand. I swam over and offered my fish. Her interest in the box and its contents was not diverted in the least when I approached. Only when she saw the fish did she turn towards me, and to my pleasure very nicely took my offering. To say 'good shark', I rubbed her nose but she turned back to the box. Obviously she wanted more food. I patted my head. This was our signal to let John Mooney, the 'on surface' assistant, know we needed more baits. It took a lot of patting before John noticed me, he was so transfixed by the tiger, but eventually he gathered his wits together and swam down with a lovely fat tuna around 15 kilos in weight. I took the fish from him and, helped by Mark Heighes our underwater assistant, fastened the tuna onto the coral. It was almost as though she knew it was hers, because she swam over immediately and with an amazing show of strength neatly ripped the fish in two. Excited by the action grey reefs dashed in from the deep, but she was boss and they kept their distance, flickering back and forth eyeing the remaining tuna hungrily. Eating the rest of the tuna proved more difficult for her as it was wired onto the coral. Unfortunately the wire went between her teeth and she could not bite through. Eventually she broke the wire and I was concerned to see about a half-metre length apparently swallowed down with the tuna. I need not have worried. To our surprise she somehow coughed the wire out which, as it had been threaded through the tuna's eyes, we found rather amazing.

By now she was swimming around and between us. On two occasions she actually bumped me, and once when I stood directly in front of her to see what would happen, she simply went over the top. I had to bend my knees to avoid a collision and ran my hand along her belly as she passed. Unlike hammerheads which are so sensitive about being touched, tigers seem to take human contact without any reaction.

The grey reef sharks followed her about, their respect for the big predator was very interesting. Once while she was feeding, a grey reef somewhat brazenly dashed in and grabbed a piece of fish. The tiger immediately swung upon the reef shark and grabbed it back straight out of the smaller shark's mouth. The established pecking order was not about to be broken.

Even when sated with tuna the tiger stayed with us. She was swimming under the boat when we eventually ran out of film and air, forcing us to leave the water.

The tiger shark was still around during the afternoon dive but stayed back watching, not coming in close like she had during the morning dive. The grey reefs were still following in single file, rather like a group of Red Indians.

Did they feel more confident staying behind, or were they hopeful she would attack some large creature which could feed them also? Perhaps it was a little of both reasons but it was interesting that the smaller whitetips practically ignored the big shark, then, they practically ignored us too, and we are also, compared to them, quite large.

The tiger episode will appear in a television production by Goldcrest called *In the Realm of the Shark*. Ron and I hope the general public, seeing how calmly our tiger shark behaved around humans both on the surface and underwater, will feel a little more kindly towards them.

The problem is our lack of understanding, not the sharks. Ron and I plan to do more work with tiger sharks. I believe I could easily tame one, making it my friend. When I do, it's going to be a great story, and if the cameras are rolling, an even greater film.

II Shark Behaviour

Shark behaviour, like child behaviour, is a subject of interest to many people. Dr Eugenie Clark has devoted many years of her life to the study of sharks and the way they behave under different situations. A diver as well as a scientist, Dr Clark has been able to observe sharks in the open ocean, which must be a great asset when studying behaviour patterns. Of course, much of her work has to be done with captive sharks. A shark in the open ocean will hardly stay around long enough for someone to photograph it, let alone conduct prolonged experiments.

It is not only the scientists and researchers who assist in the gathering of information on sharks. Anyone who observes these fish for a length of time must learn something about their behaviour patterns. For instance, big-game fishermen know that pelagic sharks favour small school fish as bait. Some game fishermen are so familiar with the way different sharks behave when hooked, that they can tell what species is on the line and roughly how much it would weigh – all this without seeing the shark and, most of the time, quite correct in their estimate.

Two different people can watch the same shark and come to two different conclusions as to what they believe the shark is doing or why he is doing it. Also there is the possibility they could both be wrong. It's going to take many more years of study before complete behaviour patterns begin to emerge. All information concerning sharks is of value, whether it comes from a famous scientist or a rock fisherman.

Ron and I have been fortunate in having spent considerable time working with grey nurse sharks (sand bar tigers in the United States). During the day, they behave in a quiet, sluggish fashion but become extremely active at night when they have to hunt for food. This is a simple observation regarding the behaviour of a certain species of shark. Although we didn't consider ourselves to be shark experts, like most experienced divers we do have a certain amount of knowledge about the behaviour of sharks we most commonly see. These simple, everyday traits of the sharks are fairly easy to define and are by now common knowledge among people who work with sharks.

The big question mark regarding shark behaviour is one asked by millions of people. Why do they attack? Nobody really knows for sure. It is a phenomenon still being studied extensively by scientists in all countries where attacks occur. It's a question that has no simple answer and I feel one that can never be answered in full.

Shark behaviour is still mostly a mystery whose surface has only been scratched. These stories I have chosen are a very mixed collection. About the only definite thing to be found by reading them is that shark behaviour is completely variable.

6
From *Sharks, Sea and Land*

Sinbad

Sharks, Sea and Land (reprinted from *Temperance World!*) is a tiny booklet, published by the Blackfriars Printing and Publishing Company in 1889. It is a collection of old stories about different sharks, including one chapter on land sharks of the human variety.

I have selected a section dealing with a shark which, like the tiger shark in the Australian shark arm case (see part VI), was instrumental in bringing a crime to the attention of the authorities. It is amazing what a shark will swallow, as the case recounted by Mr Wylie here proves.

That the attitudes of the sailor towards sharks has not changed is apparent from this story. Although the credibility of these stories leaves a lot to be desired, the old-fashioned manner of their telling makes a delightful contrast to the more serious accounts appearing in this book.

No doubt, most of the incidents related here did happen, after a fashion. Most shark stories have a true beginning. It is just that in the telling and retelling, the sharks grow longer and the men become braver.

■

Some few years ago a shark's jaw was to be seen at the Jamaica Admiralty Court. Inquiring the history of it, the following legend was told. During the great war with France in the early part of this century, our men of war had much work to do in the West Indies, as contraband of war was often carried in neutral bottoms (i.e. ships), and it was necessary that all suspicious craft should be searched. For this purpose cutters were rigged out, and junior officers placed in command, with orders to cruise and overhaul the papers of every ship they fell in with. One of these cutters, the *Sparrow* by name, was commanded by a Mr Wylie, his cruising-ground being off Cape Tiburon, a promontory on the Island of St Domingo. One day the *Sparrow* chased and overhauled an American brig, whose cargo, coupled with other circumstances, produced such a suspicion of her being enemy's property, that Wylie thought it proper to put a prize crew aboard her and sail her to Port Royal for examination.

On her arrival there the American skipper swore so positively through thick and thin, 'as only an American can', to the truth of the papers which he produced, that the court was induced to set him at liberty; thereupon the Yankee commenced a prosecution against Lieutenant Wylie, claiming demurrage for the detention of his vessel.

Whilst the case was pending, a small tender, commanded by Midshipman Titton, arrived off Port Royal. Being a friend of Wylie's he went on board the *Sparrow* and was astonished to find him 'down in the dumps' and low spirited. Inquiring the cause, he heard of the trouble his friend was in at the idea of the ruinous damages which would be awarded against him on account of the Yankee.

Titton, on hearing the name of the skipper of the brig and the nature of her cargo, told his friend to be under no apprehension, for the brig was yet a fair prize.

He then explained that, whilst cruising in his tender near the position where the *Sparrow* had chased the vessel, and much about the same time, they had caught a large shark. On its being cut open by one of the men they were surprised to hear him sing out, 'Stand by to receive your letters, my boys, for here's the postman come on board'; handing out at the same time a parcel of papers from the shark's stomach. As they were but little injured by the digestive powers of the monster, Titton retained them and the jaw as curiosities.

On comparing them with a manifest of the brig's cargo, they appeared to be the real papers of the American, which he had, when pressed in the chase, thrown overboard, and the shark had swallowed them. They proved beyond a doubt that the cargo was French.

Wylie was in high glee. The two friends proceeded at once to Kingston with this new conclusive evidence, but all further investigation was rendered unnecessary, for the skipper of the brig was so thunderstruck on hearing the circumstances (believing it to be a visitation from heaven for his perjuries) that he absconded, and the vessel after all was condemned to the *Sparrow*, with a result that Wylie got £3,000 as his share of the prize money. Titton sent up the jaw of the shark to the Admiralty Court at Jamaica with his compliments, observing that he considered it a capital collar for all neutrals to swear through in future.

THIRD fiSHERMAN: Master, I marvel how the fishes live in the sea.
FIRST fiSHERMAN: Why, as men do a-land; the great ones eat up the little ones.

Shakespeare's *Pericles*

My readers have already heard that sharks will swallow any kind of garbage,but I fear the following will be too much for their credulity, although affirmed by several well-known names: Ruysch, one of the most trustworthy of the old naturalists, writes 'that a man in mail (*Homo loricatus* he calls him) was found in the stomach of a white shark.' Blumenback, one of the most celebrated naturalists of modern times, records that in one case a whole horse was found, and Basil Hall, an eminent naval officer, relates that from the stomach of a white shark, which he saw caught, there was taken the whole skin of a buffalo, besides a quantity of other articles which had been dropped overboard in the course of the previous week. There is also a story told at St James, St Helena, of a shark having been stranded, and on the fishermen opening it, they were horrified to find the body of a full-dressed artilleryman.

The French name for shark is *requin*. As my readers are doubtless aware, this word is probably derived from the Latin *requiem*, and signifies that if a man fall into the sea among sharks, his comrades may repeat for him the usual prayers for the dead. It is seldom, if ever, that a man who is so luckless as to fall amongst shark appears again; a shriek is heard, a moving mass is seen under the surface and a fin above it; the next wave that breaks against the ship-side is crimsoned, and the horror-stricken seamen know that their messmate has gone to that bourne from which no traveller has returned.

Ancient mariners had a superstition that the spirits of their departed messmates entered into the bodies of the stormy petrels, or Mother Carey's chickens.

That white sharks have very large mouths, and, if not capable of taking in a whole horse or buffalo, are sufficiently large to take in a man, is proved by the following: H.M.S. *Flora* was, some years ago, stationed at the island of St Helena, and one day a monster shark was caught. The jaws, after the head had been severed from the body, were cleaned and opened to their fullest extent, when they were found capable of taking in the head, shoulders, and body of a lieutenant, a man of twelve stone, without touching any part of him.

The following is a descriptive account of the capture of a shark, as related by M. L. Platt in the *Musée des Sciences*.

A shark of great size, certainly not less than thirty-five feet in length, had ventured to draw near our vessel. As we were then becalmed, and had nothing to do, we hailed the pleasant burst of excitement, the agreeable relief to our monotonous occupations, which he was likely to afford us. By way of precaution, and to keep him occupied, we flung to him a pair of old boots, which he conscientiously swallowed. However, he as yet required no enticement; for while the calm lasted, and so long as our ship did not make more than three or four knots per hour, the shark never stirred from the wake of our floating palace, where he always expected to see something regal allotted to him.

While he amuses himself in plunging and diving in the wake of the ship, everybody is in a state of tumult upon deck. We arrange our warlike engines, and make ready for the battle. An enormous fish-hook is attached, by means of a bit of iron chain, to the extremity of a long, stout cable. The bait is a large piece of pork, just such another piece as the monster has already swallowed, while it lay soaking in the sea water in readiness for the crew's dinner.

At length all is ready. The captain holds in his grasp a well-greased harpoon; the slip-knots of the cable glide with complete ease, and are disposed within reach of the hand. Everybody has collected on the quarter-deck, a sailor flings the hook into the sea, and the fishing begins.

The shark now ceases to plunge and wheel about the ship, he smells the bait and lazily swims towards the floating piece of pork. He has learned long ago that so small a prey cannot escape him. Immediately that he touches it with his snout, he turns on his side, opens his huge mouth, and swallows it. But at this moment the cable is violently jerked, forcing the fish hook into one of his jaws; two hands catch firm hold of the rope, and begin to tighten it, while the shark plunges about in pain, churning the waters into foam. Sometimes the hook breaks; in such case the game must be recommenced. The shark, with torn and bleeding throat, nevertheless swallows a second bait with equal avidity.

As soon as we are satisfied that the hook is securely fixed, we draw the animal alongside; the man placed at the post of honour – generally, as in the present case, the captain – vigorously darts the harpoon into his body. It is necessary that the iron should so far penetrate into the flesh that the movable portion form a cross with the axis of the lance. We have two points of attachment, and raise the shark out of the water by means of the cable of the fish-hook and the rope of the harpoon, drawing upon both simultaneously. The animal once lifted from the sea loses a part of his strength, his fins and tail have no longer any point of support. Nothing is easier, while he hangs by the ship's side, than to pass a running bowline round his tail. The three ropes which now hold him fast run quickly over pulleys fixed to the yard-arms, and the shark is speedily landed upon the quarter-deck.

The prisoner captured, his punishment is not long delayed. In vain are all his struggles; in vain the repeated and heavy blows of his tail, which threaten to crush through the planks. A sailor plunges a hand-spike into his throat, to hold him down, while another severs his tail with an axe. In this mutilated condition he is perfectly harmless and powerless, though a blow from his tail would kill a man, or, at all events break his thigh. The monster rendered defenceless, we cut open the belly and extract the heart, which is immediately thrown overboard. Sometimes a portion of the stomach is put aside to be eaten; sometimes the animal is stripped of its skin, which is dried, while the dorsal spine is fashioned into a handsome walking-stick. The liver, also, will probably be utilized, being rich in iodized oil.

As we are now on the subject of shark-catching, the following may interest my readers as showing a novel way of destroying sharks. Reverting to the years 1847-49, whilst stationed on the West Coast of Africa in H.M.S. *Blazer*, the shark afforded many hours of amusement to the officers and men in the dreary monotonous days when no sail in sight appeared for us to go in chase of, and hopes of prize-money had gone. On one occasion the ship was anchored off Lagos, in the Gulf of Guinea, where the sharks were so numerous that the act of a man showing his face over the side of a ship apparently brought them to the surface, and to have fallen overboard would have been instant death. One morning the crew were practising with ball cartridge, when it occurred to the commanding officer that Jack Shark might form a good target, so directions were given for an 8-pound piece of Queen's own (pork) to be suspended from the foreyard arm to within two feet of the water. The ruse answered admirably, causing the greatest excitement. The monsters in quick succession rose one after the other and attempted to seize the bait, ever failing to do so, and in return getting a musket ball through the head. The sport was stirring, and gave the men something to laugh and talk about over their salt horse and weevily biscuits at mealtimes.

Sailors have an idea that the shark will not touch a black man, no doubt from the fearless manner he has of jumping overboard, sharks or no sharks in sight. The British Consul, however, at that desolate place, Lagos, said that scarcely a week passed without some natives being taken away by them, when their canoes were capsized on the bars.

At Greytown, Nicaragua, a dismal place in another quarter of the globe, where leave was prohibited to seamen, from its unhealthiness and the tempting grog-shops, houses held by a class of land sharks, it was customary for one watch (forty men) at a time of the crew of the sloop of war stationed there to be allowed to land for a run on the opposite side of the harbour, taking with them a large well-fitted shark hook, a coil of two-and-a-half-inch rope, and a log of wood for a buoy. Sharks and alligators abounded in that (now closed) harbour. To the left point of the entrance, which is sandy and steep too, like

Dungeness Point, our jolly tars would repair, light their pipes, and bait the hook with the invariable Queens' own, a little less rancid than the African rations. When ready, the baited hook, buoyed and fastened to the two-and-a-half-inch rope, would be cast into the water, the current taking it off the point. Presently the buoy would disappear for a second or two. Jack's excitement was intense, and at the boatswain's mate's piping 'Stand by', each would lay hold of the rope, allowing it to slip through his fingers as the shark tugged at the bait. On the buoy disappearing altogether, 'Haul taut' was piped, and then 'Haul away'. In a minute or two a monster of a shark was, much against its will, hauled well up on to dry land out of the water. Pipe 'Belay' was sounded, and three cheers given. The men, frantic with delight, surrounded the captive, soon cutting it up into small pieces, which were thrown into the sea for the alligators to devour.

7
From *Lord of the Sharks*

Franco Prosperi

The contradictory opinions regarding shark behaviour presented as fact by different shark experts must quickly become apparent to anyone reading this book. In his book *Lord of the Sharks*, Franco Prosperi comments on these differences of opinion.

Naturally enough, being a diver myself, I tend to side with Hans Hass, whose work appears later in this book, regarding the ferociousness of sharks; generally speaking they are not dangerous. Pechuel-Loesche's claims, which will sound to the average reader like a figment of that learned gentleman's imagination, are undoubtedly true. I have often found myself in the water surrounded by whaler sharks and, provided no provocation is initiated, they have, after the first curious examination, gone about their business without confrontation.

Francis Day's observations that shark bites inflicted on fishermen in India are usually caused when the captured sharks are hauled aboard the fishing boats before they have died are perfectly logical and, no doubt, completely factual. I know two Australian spearfishermen, and have heard of many more, who have been bitten by a supposedly dead shark. These bites are rarely severe, but still give fuel to the theory that sharks are attackers of man.

One young man was propping open the jaws of a speared and supposedly dead shark with his knife. The shark twitched, the knife slipped, and the jaws snapped shut on the unfortunate man's hand. A most unpleasant experience, but hardly the fault of the shark. However, the newspaper headlines read, DIVER MAULED BY SHARK.

Lord of the Sharks is an interesting book all around and covers many aspects of sharks and their behaviour. I liked the way Franco Prosperi tested Hass's 'scream theory'. It is interesting that his results were similar to the results I achieved when I tested the same theory.

■

Here is what several authors have had to say on the subject in the past.

First of all let us take that great eighteenth-century traveller George

Dixon, who spent a long time in the Pacific and especially among the South Sea Islands. He assures us that thereabouts the shark is not much feared, and says he once witnessed a fight between some Sandwich Islanders and a few sharks over the remains of some pork that the sailors on his ship had thrown into the sea. (This proves that sharks are not the only famished creatures.)

Gesner, however, writing in the sixteenth century, had been less optimistic. His contention was that sharks were certainly man-eaters and that, at any rate, in the tropics, one should never swim in deep water for fear of meeting them. He also quoted the case of a blue shark captured near Marseilles which was found to contain a complete soldier fully armed (an antimilitarist shark, no doubt).

Even a much more recent author, E. G. Boulenger, director of the Zoological Society's Aquarium in London, believes that certain species such as the great white shark attack man, and points out that since the Suez Canal was made these species have come into the Mediterranean, and there are always one or two casualties in the course of the season there among incautious bathers.

But swelling the throng of those who want to rehabilitate the shark and give it once more an honoured place in animal society, whitewashing its unsavoury reputation, is Pechuel-Loesch, an adventurous writer who has published the interesting experiences he has had in the course of several voyages on whalers in the South Atlantic. He declares that the shark is utterly harmless to man. When swimming he often found himself surrounded by sharks, but neither he nor the people with him ever had the slightest bother with them. He also tells that in the islands of Mocha, off the coast of Chile, the local boys, almost completely submerged and armed with strong harpoons, caught coastal sharks as they swam near the shore. As a rule the sharks were not very big, but from time to time there would be a *Carcharias* two or three yards long in their catch.

After a personal experience in the waters of Singapore, to which he has added various other accounts collected in the same area, the naturalist Sir James Alexander infers that sharks are man-eaters and extremely dangerous to bathers even in shallow water. One day he was looking for shellfish in the shallows near a coral reef by the coast when he was suddenly attacked by a school of tiger sharks, and certainly would have been overcome by their repeated assaults if a passing boat had not picked him up just in time. During the fight he lost one boot, part of his trousers, and a piece of his skin was torn off.

Francis Day, on the other hand, covering more or less the same area as Alexander, has made a most interesting and thorough study of the fishes of India and reached completely different conclusions. This writer says that although sharks are much feared by the local fishermen, he never heard of a verifiable case of death caused by the attack of a shark. It is his belief that the sinister reputation sharks have in all the coastal villages is chiefly due to the bites and wounds they inflict after they have been caught, in the confined space of the local fishing vessels, on to which they are hauled before they are dead.

The theories of many other authorities such as Risso, Maast, Couch, Rondelet, etc., might be quoted. But we would be no nearer to forming a clear idea of the behaviour of these animals.

Needless to say, all these accounts have only a relative value; they are hardly ever based on direct experience. The writer has almost never been present personally at the events he records, but is working on vague hearsay, yarns, and legends, seldom confirmed by witnesses, and some of them barely credible.

Fishermen and sailors on every coast and from every land blindly believe the tales that are passed down from one generation to another, and all of them express the most unmitigated hatred of sharks and tell the most horrifying tales about them. But if one presses them for proof, or for exact information, regarding the tragic incidents they describe, one is very unlikely to get anything from them but vague and unsubstantiated answers.

The fact of the matter is that very little is known about the habits of these animals, and that the name they have for cruelty and ferocity encourages loose writing about them. But at the turn of the last century and in the early years of this, when organized shark fishing began, knowledge concerning the shark became less superficial.

The classic exponent of this new category of fishermen is Captain William E. Young. In his famous work *Shark! Shark!*, he describes experiences he has had with sharks in practically every sea. And he too sides with the writers who unhesitatingly condemn sharks as man-eaters. Impelled by an innate aversion to these savage 'tigers of the sea' (as he himself calls them), he has devoted his entire life to hunting them.

But perhaps 'aversion' is not the right word. There is never any hatred or repulsion in the hunter when he kills his prey. This is how he describes his first encounter with sharks: 'There they were, the savage, armoured sea tigers which had become my fetish, my totem. I thrilled to the sight, as I leaned there, staring in utter fascination, my throat contracted. Tingling shivers ran up and down my spine, to my fingertips and toes. I wished for a harpoon, a rifle, anything that would give me a chance to make my first shark kill.'

Just as the true hunter will often have an exaggerated idea of the value and cleverness of the game he pursues, so does Captain Young see the ferocity and implacability of his prey a little larger than life. He cannot bear anyone to doubt the dangerousness of these lords of the sea, or to think it possible to escape safely from waters infested by them. And indeed he quotes the cases of many swimmers, of whose foolish audacity he disapproves, who never came back from bathing in ill-famed waters. His book is illustrated with horrifying photographs (at any rate in the French edition) of men trapped in those terrible jaws, and he quotes many sensational legends current in the Polynesian Islands of death due to sharks. After so many years' travel and experience, the conclusion he has come to is that sharks attack and eat man, and that to believe the contrary is both false and foolish.

Refraining for the moment from any comment, I pass on to the opinions of Dr. Hans Hass, the well-known marine scientist and one of the pioneers of underwater fishing.

His own passionate interest in the subject has aroused a worldwide interest in marine life, the fascination of which was originally revealed by William Beebe, after he had explored the coral reefs of the Pacific. Hass has been the great popularizer of underwater fishing, the love of which is now widespread among European swimmers. After an early expedition to the Caribbean, he has continued his field work in the Red Sea and the Mediterranean, with particular emphasis on photography.

In these expeditions of his, which started one year before World War II, he frequently met sharks. It was the first time that man had found himself in the shark's own environment, at the mercy of its attacks, which it was thought nobody could resist, with nothing in his hands but a camera and a long harpoon. So that Hass's evidence on this enthralling subject was of paramount importance. Actually Hass did not propose to carry out a scientific investigation of the subject, but nevertheless his testimony is extremely valuable.

What happened the first time Hans Hass found himself gazing into the eyes of a 'sea tiger'? Nothing much: for a little while man and beast stared at each other, then they both went their several ways each equally anxious to come safely out of the unusual encounter. But things did not always go so smoothly: sometimes the sharks would lunge dangerously and cause some most unpleasant thrills.

One day Hass and two members of his expedition were hard pressed in just such a situation, when they made an accidental discovery: the terrified cries of one of the party, reverberating in the water, put the shark to flight as though it could not bear the intensity of the unexpected vibrations caused by the latter which affect the shark's abnormally sensitive receiving organs, and utterly terrify it.

But it isn't always as simple as it sounds. When we ourselves tried to put the advice of these Austrians into practice, we didn't always get what we wanted.

After experimenting with the scream theory under water (both when it seemed necessary and when it didn't), with a considerable number of sharks belonging to the various dangerous species, we decided that the terror we aroused was in proportion to the size of the animal.

That is to say, if the shark was young and small, not more than four or five feet in length, one could count on a scream putting it to instant flight, but with the bigger sharks, especially the ones over six or seven feet, it was a very different matter. The animal felt our vibrations, and would shy abruptly every time we screamed, but this did not make it go away, nor stop lunging. The only result of the screams was to irritate it and make it weave around us faster.

To sum up, Hans Hass asserts that a good underwater fisherman, especially if he has a friend with him, so that a lookout is kept for other unexpected attacks, should not be afraid of meeting these lords of the deep. His conclusion, it will be seen, is the exact opposite of Captain Young's.

Naturally as Hass's views are the result of direct observation and of his own personal experience in the shark's natural habitat, they are of far greater value to us than the frequently secondhand accounts reported by Young, Gesner, Alexander, Henglin, and Risso, who all more or less agree in considering the shark as a man-eater. Dixon, Pechuel-Loesch, Day, and Wyatt Gill, on the other hand, agree with Hass.

We may reduce the problem to the simple question: 'Is the shark dangerous to man or is he not?' But there is no simple answer. All sorts of different conditions may bring about different results when man meets shark. Place, time, and the species of the animal may all be determining factors.

8

The Vanishing Grey Nurse

Valerie Taylor

I wrote 'The Vanishing Grey Nurse' for the *Australian Women's Weekly*. Over the years, they have published many of my shark stories, so that I have been able to present the conservation angle to a large number of people.

As always, when I write of sharks being rather nice creatures, not nasty, vicious, man-eating monsters, I receive a sudden flow of letters from readers. Usually, the letters supporting my viewpoint outnumber those condemning what I have said.

'The Vanishing Grey Nurse' created more interest than usual. As I thought it a very ordinary little story, I was surprised at the large amount of mail. I think that it was because every year, in Australia, several people are bitten by sharks. We are probably the most shark-conscious people in the world, and much is made, by the media, of each attack.

Almost always the shark is described as being grey in colour. This is not surprising, as most sharks are some shade of grey. So, because of his name, the gentle grey nurse *(Odontaspis taurus)* has become the grey attacker of man to many people.

It is probably for this reason that the article caused so much interest. I had letters from mothers telling me that I was mistaken. One sweet lady used three pages explaining to me that if I didn't change my view I would end up a grey nurse's breakfast. A schoolteacher used it constructively, reading the article to her class of ten-year-olds, and following with an hour's discussion on the points raised.

Most who criticized objected to my describing the grey nurse as timid, harmless creatures saying that I was giving people the wrong impression. I believe that my assessment is correct. There are many hundreds of species of shark and the grey nurse is only one of them. It is a pity that the aggressive actions of a few species are attributed to a shark which would never attack without extreme provocation.

■

Making an acceptable television series is not easy and making one about a particular species of shark in its natural element is, at times, almost impossible. Without years of diving experience, it would be impossible. Ten years ago, large fish life – sharks, rays, groupers – abounded all along the coast of New South Wales. The water was clear, too.

Now, pollution and spearfishing have both taken a tremendous toll. A toll that only someone who has been diving a long time could know. It is unfortunate that newcomers to the sport will never fully realize what they have missed.

Former Australian spearfishing champion Vic Ley, Ron, and myself have recently finished working along the east coast, completing the last of our TV shows. One episode, called The 'Vanishing Grey Nurse', could almost have been retitled 'The Vanished Grey Nurse'. Without our library of stock shots, this episode would have been impossible. The large schools of grey nurse sharks have vanished.

The reason is not hard to find. I can remember seeing a well-known Queensland diver powerhead (an explosive-headed spear, fired from a rubber-powered spear gun) twenty-two grey nurses at Seal Rocks one sunny day nine years ago. He seemed to think he was a superhero and strutted up and down boasting of his great deed. If swimming up to a peaceful unsuspecting creature resting in a gutter and blowing its brains out with a shotgun cartridge makes a hero, I guess he was. In those days, grey nurse were considered to be man-eaters, but even so, the sight of all those sad grey bodies drifting back and forth in the surge was sickening.

Twelve years ago, the grey nurse was blamed for most shark attacks in Australian waters. We genuinely believed we were hunting true man-eaters and brave was the diver who, armed with only a conventional spear gun, sought out these vicious murderers in their own element. The invention of the powerhead served to accelerate the indiscriminate slaughter, but many divers, ourselves included, realized that the grey nurse shark seemed extremely unaggressive and was, in all likelihood, the victim of false publicity. However, killing sharks had become a popular sport.

Whether the hunted was dangerous or not made no difference, it was the name *shark* that counted. Only the lack of available victims has finally slowed the slaughter down.

Nowadays, anyone who thinks grey nurse sharks are dangerous, savage beasts, and that to kill one makes the victor some kind of superhero, needs his marbles rearranged.

During our weeks of searching, the few sharks we did find were in deep water off isolated reefs or islands. They were so afraid of divers that it was almost impossible to film them. Although we didn't plan it this way, the vanishing grey nurse is the story of tragedy, or to put it more bluntly, a story of man's stupidity. We show how it was, what we did, and how it is now. A common enough theme in today's civilized world.

Ron and I are not innocent either, and to say I killed only a few is no excuse. Our punishment was making this film, knowing what we had done and suffering for it, as we searched the barren surge-swept gutters. It cost us money and precious time, but more distressing was knowing that we had played a part, however small, in the slaughter.

At Nine Mile Reef off the New South Wales–Queensland border, we found no sharks. Solitary Islands, out from Wooli, New South Wales, were devoid, not only of sharks but almost anything else as well. The gutters at Fish Rock, New South Wales, were also empty, though we had a fleeting glimpse of one lonesome shark in very deep water around the back of the rock.

Further south, at Mermaid Reef, where Vic had seen dozens of grey nurse only a few years before, one frightened shark was sighted and it swam away never to be seen by us again. We had already been to Brush Island and Montague Island further south.

Seal Rocks, 200 miles north of Sydney, was to be the last area we would search. For the first time since we had started filming the series, six cyclone-studded months before, really good weather moved in, from the north-east.

We arrived at Seal Rocks on 6 April 1973, late in the afternoon. Although a big swell was running, we decided to launch our dinghy and do a quick reconnaissance of what we felt to be the most likely places to find sharks.

The first place we looked was in the old shark gutter, the same place that superhero conducted his big slaughter nine years before. I really expected to find nothing so when Vic, who had gone in for a quick look, surfaced and said, 'There is a shark down there,' I was not prepared at all.

There was a big scramble for gear, cameras, and lights. We had to work fast. Already it was late afternoon. Ron was in the water, lights and all, in about ten minutes. I was not far behind. Underwater visibility was roughly 50 feet, but close to the rock where we had anchored, foam caused by the breaking waves cut that distance in half. The shark was hard to see. He blended into the grey rocks and I did not notice him until he moved.

When he saw us he turned and swam away. This shark did not seem afraid of us. He was only a baby. Six feet long and about one year old. (Jack Evans, the owner of the Porpoise Pool at Tweed Heads, has two grey nurse who were actually born in his tank. They were six feet long when a year old.)

We followed the little shark up the gutter. Even down 20 feet, visibility was poor. With what seemed like deliberate casualness, the shark ignored us. We moved without haste. As we neared the rock, the entrance to a cave grew blackly through the haze. Our shark vanished inside, becoming as one with the darkness. We followed. To our amazement, thirteen baby grey nurse sharks materialized in the gloom, beautiful creatures drifting together in complete harmony. I was tremendously excited.

Ron and Vic began filming. It was instantly obvious that the sharks found Ron's camera lights upsetting, for they flicked aside as he approached, thumping their tails loud in the confined space. As we moved further into the cave, one by one, the sharks left, swimming silently away. Delighted with our good fortune we followed, but they had scattered among the tumbled rocks. Ron found one in deeper water and spent some time stalking her, but she was clearly nervous and kept her distance. It was hopeless for my photography so I decided to swim back for another look at the cave, while Ron and Vic hunted around in the deeper water. As I neared the cave entrance I saw a little shark sneaking back. Then, from the turbulent shallows above the cave, another shark appeared and slipped silently into his home. It was rather like playing hide-and-seek – five sharks were already home and within minutes two more arrived. They had certainly given the boys the slip.

Poor little babies, all they wanted was to be left in peace. I could almost see the worried look being sent in my direction as I swam closer. The agitation in the cave seemed to increase, but as long as I stayed outside the sharks remained together. I turned to see Ron approaching with his camera and the lights which disturbed them greatly. A courageous male left the group, swam toward Ron, almost brushing me with his fins. Right up to the camera he went, then suddenly, with a whack of his tail, he was gone. Ron ran off his remaining film and we returned to our dinghy.

By the time we reached the beach, it was almost dark. Vic and Ron wrestled the dinghy through the surf and the backbreaking struggle with gear, cameras, boats, and trailer began.

It is relatively easy to manhandle a 15-foot aluminium dinghy and 40-horse Evinrude motor down a sandy beach, but quite different to manhandle it up.

We were all pleased with our afternoon's work. After so many disappointments, we finally had success. The following day was really beautiful, but the seas were still fairly heavy, which meant continued poor visibility. Two local boys were going out with us. They were interested in what we were doing and we were interested in the extra manpower when it came to beaching the boat. Also they were really nice guys and, although not divers, had a love of the sea and her creatures that matched our own. We launched the boat without any problems.

When we reached the gutter, Vic hung over the gunwhale for a quick look. There was still a lot of foam around and the surge was a nuisance. He couldn't immediately see any sharks. My heart sank a little, but Ron said, 'Get in and have a good look.' Vic simply rolled off the boat and vanished. Our guests, John and Greg, were amazed that anyone, let alone someone completely unarmed, would just swim off looking for a pack of sharks.

Ron tried to explain how placid grey nurse are by nature, but I am not sure he was believed completely. In a minute, Vic was back with the good news that our little actors were huddled up into the cave, ready and waiting for the action to start. He claimed they all frowned when he appeared and I could well believe it.

Once again we moved among the sharks and once again they, one by one, left. Actually the only difference to the action of the previous day, was that this time the sharks did not return to their cave. This pleased us, for although we appeared rather pushy in forcing the sharks to vacate their home, we really were doing them a favour. The cave was in shallow water well within the reach of skin divers, and, because of this, the little sharks were very vulnerable. A diver armed with a powerhead could easily kill four or five sharks before they realized something was wrong and swam into the safety of deeper water.

Without harming them, we had taught them that humans were nasty, annoying creatures who should be avoided. Ron had some marvellous close-ups of the sharks and I some great stills. Vic Ley, using Ron's second camera, had shot some very acceptable film of Ron and me working with the sharks.

Although we had to be in Sydney by the following evening, we planned one more quick dive before we left. I guess everyone was interested to see if the sharks had returned during the night.

We were up very early and anchored over the gutter. Vic swam down to survey the situation. There were no little sharks. He dived into deeper water. Still no sharks. Although we were not sorry they had left the shallows, Ron still needed a few more shots for the end sequence of the episode.

We sat in the boat for a while wondering where they could be. Vic knew of a cave in deep water about two miles away that he thought sharks might like. Ron decided it was worth taking a look.

We anchored over the area. Ron and Vic donned their gear and did a bump dive to the bottom to reconnoitre the place. They were back in seconds, grins all over their faces.

It seemed incredible, but the sharks were there.

Ron dropped over his lights, started the generator, and down he went. Sure enough, there they were, thirteen familiar little sharks. How they must have hated seeing the three of us again. Their new cave had two entrances: Ron swam in the large one and I squeezed through the back way, putting myself behind the sharks. This time they were not in such a hurry to leave, though the flash of my camera gave one such a fright he banged into Ron, skinning Ron's hand.

They were sharing this cave with a four-foot Port Jackson shark and several red moyongs. As caves go, it was very beautiful. The walls were coated with orange sponge and pink sea tulips hung around the entrance. Eventually, our noisy presence proved too much and, one by one, the sharks reluctantly moved out. When last I saw them, they were swimming slowly down. We followed to well over 140 feet before giving up. Somehow, I think they will return to the orange-walled cave, though I would rather they found a new home, so remote and so deep that no powerhead-wielding diver will ever find them again. Only by doing this will they be completely safe.

'The Vanishing Grey Nurse' is one of my favourite episodes in our 'Inner Space' series. Ron and I feel that anyone seeing this film cannot help but feel that the shark has rights too. More, perhaps, than we do, in the underwater world of 'inner space'.

In July 1977 I sent a letter to Dr D. Franzois, Director of Fisheries, New South Wales, describing our experiences with the grey nurse shark and the decline in their numbers. I requested that the grey nurse be protected by law from line fishermen and spearfishermen all along the coast of New South Wales. No decision has at this time been reached regarding my request.

We continued to work towards having the grey nurse protected, writing letters and making television appearances. Ron's footage showing me swimming with whole schools of supposedly dangerous grey nurse helped greatly. The divers were the first to decide they should be left alone, but this was not law, just a change of attitude among a small number of people who knew the fish in its natural element. However, it was a start, and over the years we never let pass an opportunity where we could speak out on behalf of the grey nurse.

In 1984, several weeks after speaking at the Australian Museum in Sydney about conservation, particularly that of the grey nurse shark, I received from a Dr Dave Pollard, Senior Research Scientist and acting Director of the Fisheries Research Institute of New South Wales, a letter to which was attached a government notification regarding a gazetted fishing closure whereby the taking of the grey nurse shark *(Carcharias arenarius)* and the herbst nune shark *(Carcharias herbsti)* from the water by any means whatsoever, is prohibited by law in New South Wales.

This is probably the first time any government has had the courage to protect a large well-armed shark whose reputation (though undeserved) is not a kindly one. It also proves that people are changing their outlook regarding supposedly dangerous animals, and that our efforts can eventually achieve the desired result.

9

From *The Arcturus Adventure*

William Beebe

If the name William Beebe means anything to most people, it is in connection with his deep dives in the bathysphere. But this was not his sole area of interest or claim to fame. He did a lot of the early pioneering scientific work connected with underwater exploration.

The Arcturus Adventure is an account of his experiences diving with helmet and hose – hard-hat diving. His experiences recounted here are almost identical to those we have had under similar conditions, the main difference being not in the fish life, but in the unwieldy diving equipment he was using.

Beebe's inquisitive mind and fine sense of curiosity must have played a major part in his success. He was obviously a man who went under the sea to expand human knowledge. Each dive enhanced his own understanding of fish and sharks. I thought his experiments with feeding the shark revealed he was not prepared to take anyone's word for anything. He had to see for himself.

This reflects our own approach to the sea and its creatures. We have seen for ourselves and drawn our own conclusions, which are frequently in opposition to established opinion. We think that each person should have the chance to see for himself, which is why the objective underwater films made by us and other underwater film teams are so valuable for research and teaching purposes.

■

When I rolled over and looked about, there came to me a vision of the abundance of life in the sea. The cloud of little fishes had gone, even the ubiquitous yellow-tailed surgeons were out of sight for once, and yet from where I sat I could see not fewer than seven or eight hundred fish, not counting the wrasse and gobies which played around my fingers as thickly as grasshoppers in a hayfield. Out of the blue-green distance or up from frond-draped depths, good-sized grey sharks appeared now and then. Two came slowly towards me, closer with the in-surge and then floating farther off with the out-swing. They turned first one then the other catlike eye towards me, and after a good look veered off. Near to them were playing round-headed pigfish, a few Zesurus swam still nearer, and even small scarlet snappers, the prey of almost every hungry fish or aquatic bird, even these went by without any show of nervousness. The pair of sharks passed on, almost unnoticed, and all the mass of life of this wonder world seemed going smoothly and undisturbed. Far away in the dim distance one of the sharks appeared again, or it may have been another – when, looking around me, I saw every fish vanishing. While I have mentioned what must seem an identical occurrence before, yet this was as different as a great battle is from a street accident. Through copper and glass and air I sensed some peril very unlike the former reaction to the sea lion, and I rapidly climbed a half-dozen rungs, swallowing hard as I went to adjust to the new altitude. Clinging close to the ladder I looked everywhere, but saw nothing but waving seaweed. The distant shark had vanished together with all the hosts of fish, even to the bullying, fearless groupers. I was the only living being except the starfish and the tiny waving heads of the hydroids which grew in clusters among the thinner growths of weed, as violets appear amidst high grass. Whether the distant shark was some different, very dreaded kind or whether some still more inimical thing had appeared – fearful even to the strange shark – I shall never know. Five minutes later, fear had again passed, and life, not death, was dominant.

I climbed to the surface at last, my teeth chattering from the prolonged immersion. This water, although in no sense the Humboldt Current, is much cooler than that at Cocos and I became numb and chilled without knowing it. Excitement and concentrated interest keep me keyed up, and the constant need of balance requires that every muscle is taut, and then when I reach the surface and relax, the chill seems to enter my very bones. Fortunately there is always either rowing or pumping to do and this soon warms me.

During my last dive I had noticed five or six new species of fishes and hoping to hook some of the smaller ones, I decided to get some bait. I had the boat backed near shore and at a propitious moment on the crest of one of the lesser swells I leaped off. The scarlet crabs here are remarkably tame, far more so than on any of the other islands, a fact for which I can in no way account. The casual visits of man may be of course ruled out as having nothing to do with it, and yet here birds and fish, the crab's most deadly enemies, are unusually abundant.

With two big scarlet crabs I vaulted back on the crest of another convenient little swell, fortunately just avoiding the succeeding three, any one of which would have tossed our cockle-shell high up on the jagged lava. I found to my disappointment that we had between us only one hook and that a large one. However, I anchored again near the spot where I had last dived and threw over the hook. I immediately caught one of the round-headed pigfish, about a foot in length. As I was pulling in a second one, a six-foot shark swung towards him and this gave me a hint upon which I acted at once. I pulled in the fish quickly and studied the situation through the water glass. Two sharks were swimming slowly about the very rock where I had been sitting a few minutes before, probably the same individuals who had then been so curious about me. A small group of the pigfish swam around, over and below the sharks as they had done when I was submerged, sometimes passing within a foot of the sharks' mouths without the slightest show of emotion, or fear, or otherwise. An angelfish and two yellow-tailed cows passed, and a golden grouper together with two deep green giants of the same species milled around beneath the boat, cocking their eyes up at us, now and then.

I baited the hook with a toothsome bit of crab and lowered it. All the pigfish rushed it at once, and as it descended, the sharks and groupers followed with mild interest, almost brushing against it but wary of the line. Failing to elicit any more practical attention from the golden grouper, I allowed one of the pigfish to take the bait and hook. Then, watching very carefully, I checked his downward rush, and swung him upward. He struggled fiercely and like an electric shock every shark and grouper turned towards him. Without being able to itemize any definite series of altered swimming actions, something radical had happened. The remainder of the school of pigfish, while they remained in the neighbourhood, yet gathered together in a group and milled slowly in a small circle. There was no question that from being a quiet, slowly swimming, casually interested lot of fish, the three groups – pigfish, groupers, and sharks – had become surcharged with interest focused on the fish in trouble. I drew the hooked fish close to the boat, and could plainly see that the hook has passed only around the horny maxillary. There was not a drop of blood in the water, and the disability of the fish consisted in its attachment to the line. Yet the very instant the struggle to free itself began, the groupers and sharks, from being at least in appearance friendly – or certainly wholly disregarding the pigfish – became concertedly inimical, focused upon it with the most hostile feeling of an enemy and its prey.

For half an hour I played upon this reaction and learned more than I had ever seen or read of the attacking and feeding habits of groupers and sharks. When the struggling began the sharks all turned towards the hooked fish. Not only the one nearest who must easily have seen it for himself, but two, far off, turned at the same time instant, and within a few seconds two more from quite invisible distances and different directions. What I saw seemed to prove conclusively that sharks, like vultures, watch one another and know at once when prey has been sighted by one of their fellows. The numerous sharks thus call one another all unintentionally, as when one of our party caught a shark at Cocos, and in an incredibly short time there were seventeen attacking it. On the other hand it must be admitted that sharks differ from vultures as widely as the poles in the matter of scent. Vultures all but lack this sense, while we know that fish have it well developed. But even in the case of blood in the water, it seems to me that diffusion cannot be nearly rapid enough to account for the instantaneous reaction on sharks near and far. The phenomenon is as remarkable in general aspect as the apparent materialization from the air of a host of vultures where a few minutes before none were visible.

Even more than in this problem, I was interested in the exact method of feeding of sharks and groupers. After making sure of the first phase of interest, I allowed a six-foot shark to approach the hooked pigfish. It came rather slowly, then with increased speed and finally made an ineffectual snap at the fish. The third time it seized it by the tail and with a strong sideways twist of the whole body, tore the piece off. The second fish attacked was pulled off the hook, and two sharks then made a simultaneous rush at it. So awkward were they that one caught his jaw in the other's teeth and for a moment both swished about in a vortex of foam at the side of the boat.

I noted carefully about thirty distinct efforts or attacks on the hooked fish, and only three times was I able by manoeuvring the fish to get the shark to turn even sideways, never once on its back, as the books so glibly relate. I sacrificed seven pigfish, and then tried to get the golden grouper, but it was too wary. A giant five-foot green grouper, larger than any we had taken thus far, was becoming more and more excited, however, and when I had trolled him close to the surface I let my fish lure drift loosely. One swift snap and the entire fish disappeared, then a single slight nod of the head and the line parted cleanly. The general effect was of much greater force and power exerted in a short space of time than in the case of the sharks. When it comes to lasting power for only a short time, after being landed, however, the groupers fight while the sharks smash and thrash until they are actually cut to pieces.

After this exhibition, without hesitation, I dived in the helmet again in this very spot with no change in the attitude of the sharks towards me. I had had these sharks close to me a little while before, and although my efforts under water seem to me no less awkward and helpless than a hooked pigfish, yet to these so-called man-eaters, there is apparently all the difference in the world, and I was absolutely safe from attack.

Mr Zane Grey, who, at my recommendation, went to Cocos and the Galapagos, had as his object big-game fishing, and as the following paragraphs will show, he underwent the same experience that we had, both when we were here two years ago on the *Noma*, and now again on the *Arcturus*.

Fishing off Chatham Bay, Cocos Island, he writes in his book *Tales of Fishing Virgin Seas*:

The next hour was so full of fish that I could never tell actually what did happen. We had hold of some big crevalle, and at least one enormous yellowtail, perhaps seventy-five pounds. But the instant we hooked one, great swift grey and yellow shadows appeared out of obscurity. We never got a fish near the boat. Such angling got on my nerves. It was a marvellous sight to peer down into that exquisitely clear water and see fish as thickly laid as fence pickets, and the deeper down the larger they showed. All kinds of fish lived together down there. We saw yellowtail and amberjack swim among the sharks as if they were all friendly. But the instant we hooked a poor luckless fish, he was set upon by these voracious monsters and devoured. They fought like wolves. Whenever the blood of a fish discoloured the water these sharks seemed to grow frantic. They appeared on all sides, as if by magic.

By and by we had sharks of all sizes swimming round under our boat. One appeared to be about twelve feet long or more, and big as a barrel. There were only two kinds, the yellow sharp-nosed species; and the bronze shark with black fins, silver-edged. He was almost as grand as a swordfish.

While trying to get the big fellow to take a bait I hooked and whipped three of his bunch, the largest one being about two hundred and fifty pounds. It did not take me long to whip them, once I got a hook into their hideous jaws. The largest, however, did not get to my bait.

An interesting and gruesome sight was presented when Bob, after dismembering one I had caught, tumbled the bloody carcass back into the water. It sank. A cloud of blood spread like smoke. Then I watched a performance that beggared description. Sharks came thick upon the scene from everywhere. Some far down seemed as long as our boat. They massed around the carcass of their slain comrade, and a terrible battle ensued. Such swift action, such ferocity, such unparalleled instinct to kill and eat! But this was a tropic sea, with water at eighty-five degrees, where life is so intensely developed. Slowly that yellow flashing, churning mass of sharks faded into the green depths.

10

From *Sharks and Other Ancestors*

Wade Doak

Walter Starck's inventiveness and dedication has opened some of the sea's once closed doors. Nothing is too bizarre or small for Walter to investigate – his studies of sea snakes and sunworshippers in the Pacific led him to band his wetsuit as a shark protection. This was one of his better-known experiments and involved painting white horizontal stripes on his black wetsuit in an effort to frighten sharks away. The idea behind this odd action was that sharks were supposedly afraid of sea snakes, some of which are banded.

Using Dr Starck's research vessel, *El Torito*, as a base, Wade Doak spent many months diving in tropical areas inhabited by these sharks. His book, *Sharks and Other Ancestors*, describes in detail many of his personal encounters with sharks both dangerous and placid. These are the sort of encounters which eventually happen to any diver who consistently works in the remote reef areas of the Indo-Pacific.

A fine underwater photographer and writer, New Zealander Wade Doak writes about the grey reef shark with an authority that comes only from personal experience.

The grey reef shark, because of its aggressive personality and the fact that in virgin areas it is generally numerous has become a popular subject for both underwater photographers and thrill-seeking spear-fishermen. The latter hunt the sharks with explosive-tipped spears for little more than the excitement of the kill. It is easy to see, from Doak's descriptions of the grey sharks, why they make such good photo-graphic material. They are also excellent subjects for scientific research. Dr Starck has been studying grey reef sharks in their natural habitat for many years.

After the initial burst of publicity, little more has been heard about the striped wetsuit and it would appear that the idea has not been pursued – which, considering the lack of banded sea snakes in most of the world's oceans, is probably just as well.

Anyone interested in learning more about sharks and their behaviour in their natural element would find Doak's book interesting reading. It is obvious that he has had personal experience with the different marine animals he writes about, which makes a refreshing change from the exaggerated viciousness and danger writers with less experience usually attribute to large marine creatures.

Since writing this introduction in 1978, I have extensively tested Dr Starck's banded wet suit theory at different locations in both the Northern Indian Ocean and south-west Pacific. never have I found sharks to be such a problem. The suit seemed to work in reverse. Sharks loved me. On several occasions I found myself beating normally timid sharks, such as the grey reef, away with my bare hands. Their persistence was astounding. It was almost as though they could not see me. I tested stripes both three inches (7·5cm) and two inches (5cm) in width with the same alarming results. The sharks acted almost as though they could not see me and even when hit several times, were reluctant to move away.

Like Starck, I used baits to attract the sharks initially, but where my threatening (to them) presence normally would keep the marauders at a distance, when wearing the banded suits, they approached without hesitation or fear.

My outfits were sports suits made of two-way stretch lycra. With only this thin material between me and the sharks, I felt very vulnerable indeed.

■

One of the most graceful and streamlined of the reef sharks, the grey is also one of the most widespread and abundant species around coral reefs and atolls. They often gather in passes where there are dense masses of fish, and dozens of individuals may be seen cruising up and down ready to attack any fish which shows signs of stress.

Up to eight feet in length but usually around five feet, this reef shark is uniformly dark grey, except for the whitish stomach and the black tinge on the trailing edges of its fins. This is especially marked on the upper lobe of the caudal.

The teeth of the upper jaw are broadly triangular; those of the lower jaw narrower. The upper teeth have serrated edges, the serrations more pronounced on the posterior edges of the teeth. The lower teeth have smooth edges. This tooth pattern is an ideal compromise for an all-purpose predator. The narrow, smooth lower teeth are for grasping and holding slippery active prey while the heavier, serrated upper teeth are adapted for cutting up the prey and chopping chunks from larger food items.

The tooth pattern is similar in silvertips and blacktips; the whitetip has tricuspid teeth and is more specialized for catching and holding small fishes without the heavy teeth for cutting up larger prey.

Of the reef sharks the grey is the most dangerous to man. A book on the fishes of Polynesia reports ten recent attacks by greys in French Polynesia alone. One resulted in death, another required amputation, and the others produced deep, semicircular, crenellated wounds, with torn muscles, blood haemorrhage, and deep shock requiring rapid treatment.

At Eniwetok in the Marshall Islands Richard Johnson and Donald Nelson, two diving scientists, carried out a series of experiments on grey reef sharks to determine whether they would make attacks on man for reasons other than feeding. Until then the basic assumption in shark deterrent research has been that sharks are motivated to attack men chiefly by hunger. From the new research and Walt Starck's studies it seems apparent that while this may be the case with the largest species such as tiger sharks and white sharks, it is not true for others, especially grey sharks. Greys often compete for food, and have developed a ritualized threat display which is likely to be of communicative value in their normal social encounters with each other and other shark species. (Just as a dog will raise its hackles and bare its teeth as a threat gesture, and only attack if the threat is ignored.)

It has long been believed sharks would not attack scuba divers when there was nothing to arouse their feeding responses: no blood in the water or wounded fish. However, with increased diving activity in the Pacific and the pooling of information, it is now clear that this is not true. Of the many reported attacks on scuba and skin divers by grey sharks, none involves the shark feeding on his victim. They all bite and run.

Johnson and Nelson analyzed such reports and discovered there were several factors common to each attack which deserved investigation. Often the diver reported preliminary behaviour such as in this account by Ron Church: 'The shark started in a small circle just opposite us and as he came around, his body started turning and twisting and rolling back and forth in the water as he swam. The whole body was being used to swim with, his head moving back and forth almost as much as his tail. He trimmed himself with his pectorals.'

The scientist noted reports of five incidents where such behaviour led to attacks on men. They then looked for any factors common to these attacks which might explain their provocation. They found that in each case the shark had found its escape route restricted in some way by the divers.

In the case above, Ron Church said the shark had passed between the two divers and the reef wall. The divers had moved towards the shark as it passed and this had apparently released the behaviour pattern described. As soon as the threat display was complete the shark rapidly dashed at one of the divers, Jim Stewart, who received two severe bites just above the elbow.

In shark literature it has often been recommended that if a shark seems a menace the diver should stand his ground and act aggressively towards it. This may hold true for big lone predators such as tiger sharks, but it is most dangerous with the reef sharks.

With considerable courage Johnson and Nelson set up a series of experiments on grey sharks to determine and record on film just what the pattern of threat behaviour was and to see if it could be provoked by a diver. They conducted a series of ten tests in which a diver (carrying a means of defence which would undoubtedly have been useless), upon seeing an approaching grey shark, swam rapidly at it from twenty feet range. In each of the ten trials the shark made a definite threat display. This lasted from fifteen seconds to one minute and varied in intensity according to the degree to which it was cornered or restricted from escape by different types of reef structure.

As a control the divers did another series of tests where, upon the approach of the shark, the diver made no movement towards it. In every such case the shark made no threat display and left without attacking.

Clearly, if a diver, either by accident or intent, surprises a grey shark and moves towards it aggressively, he risks triggering a pattern of ritualized behaviour likely to end in attack, especially if the shark finds its escape routes restricted.

From analysis of slow-speed movie frames, the scientists found the threat display was as follows: the shark begins to swim in an S-shaped path, elongate at first, intensifying to a figure of eight pattern as it gets closer to the diver, doubling back on its course and holding its ground. It swims with an exaggerated lateral motion, its body rolling or spiral looping, the pectoral fins severely depressed. The shark's body is gripped with extreme muscular tension, the snout raised, jaws slightly open, and back arched. It is making an instinctive threat gesture to counter the aggressive approach of the diver. Such ritualized behaviour must have developed under natural conditions for use in courtship or territorial defence, but in the case of wide-ranging sharks the term *Lebensraum* or living space is more apt than the idea of a precise geographical territory. Many fishes use fin displays and exaggerated swimming movements for threat display against rivals and much the same behavioural pattern is used in courtship.

Walt has used the *El Torito*'s wet submarine to carry such studies further. With its speed, manoeuvrability, and protection, he has been able to observe provoked attacks by grey sharks on repeated occasions. Once the propellor was seized and the drive pin snapped, necessitating an ascent without power. Another time a shark broke one of the half-inch plastic windows in the rear canopy.

Walt told me that the first grey reef shark attack on the submarine occurred when *El Torito* was at Eniwetok, Marshall Islands.

We were cruising along the seaward side of the atoll near the outer drop-off, in about seventy feet of water. It was the first day that we'd taken the submarine out to actually use it in the Pacific. Visibility was around 150 feet when we spotted this grey about eighty feet ahead. A large individual for a grey, he was close to seven feet long. His attack behaviour was typical of that we saw in subsequent encounters; as we approached him at a distance of perhaps forty feet, he began to swim with a slightly exaggerated lateral motion of the head. This increased as the submarine began to catch up with him. At about twenty-five feet distance, he began to arch his back slightly about two-thirds of the way along, which gave him a rather stiff-bodied appearance. At the same time his pectoral fins angled downward. Instead of being held out to the sides horizontally, they angled down at a 45-degree angle. He was swimming with this stiff-bodied motion, pectorals down, head wagging side to side and moving away from us.

As the sub continued to gain on him, at a distance of perhaps twenty feet, he suddenly whirled and made a rapid circle around to our left and attacked the propeller from behind. The circle was so fast that if you'd been in the water it would have been virtually impossible to turn around and face him as quickly as he came around. Still moving fast, he came in, hit the propeller, and sheared the drive pin so the motor suddenly revved up. The submarine lost speed and sank to the bottom. He then circled around looking like he might attack again. We didn't have any side windows on then and I was really afraid that he might charge in. If he hit where the window gaps were, he might end up inside, which would be disastrous. Fortunately he didn't and we sat still until he went away. I blew the ballast tanks and came to the surface. When we got back to the island with the sub, I found an old plastic desktop, cut it up and made the side windows that are on now.

My first thought was that his attack had been directed at the noise and motion of the propeller. However, the next attack occurred in a lagoon pass with a very similar pre-attack pattern. This time the shark first attacked the body of the submarine and then returned to attack the canopy right at our faces. In all he made five separate attacks. He'd hit in and bounce off and I'd turn the sub and go after him and he'd attack it again. Subsequent attacks involved both the body of the sub and the canopy. The latter seemed to be directed at us inside but, of course, glanced off the clear plastic instead.

In between these attacks there were a number of sharks we approached which didn't attack. I would say one out of five sharks attacks, and the others just tend to move away with a stiff-bodied motion, managing to swim just a little faster than we're moving.

In a couple of striking instances, the pre-attack display became so exaggerated they lost all forward motion in the water and ended up suspended at a 45-degree angle, slashing their heads back and forth, snapping their jaws with pectorals down and back arched. The whole motion is similar to what they do when they are tearing into a large prey to rip a chunk out of it. So I think this pre-attack may really be a displaced attack, which, in some instances, is carried through to an actual attack. There's a desire to repel a competitor or something that's threatening them but also the opposing drive to attack is displaced by fear. But if the drive to attack becomes strong enough to overcome the opposing fear then the attack is carried out on the sub.

There doesn't seem to be anything that directs it at any one part of the sub; it's been at the canopy or us inside, it's been at the fibreglass body of the sub and it's been at the propeller.

The last attack was at Kuop. We were cruising beside a vertical drop-off along the wall of the pass at a depth of about ninety feet. Suddenly I felt something hit the sub. My first thought was that I'd bumped an outcropping of coral rock with a wingtip. I quickly glanced over. It was simply a quick, natural response: I felt a bump and glanced over because I thought I'd been hit. I could see I was about five feet off the wall.

I looked back – Al Giddings, the underwater photographer, was in the back seat. He shrugged and looked at me. I thought something had dropped back there – maybe his tank or camera had bumped something. But Al just shrugged and looked at me – and we went along a little way, perhaps thirty feet, when suddenly there was another bump. At this point we were well out from the wall, perhaps ten feet or so. I felt right then that it must be a shark, but I hadn't seen any. There wasn't one ahead of us or above us – apparently it was below us and I couldn't see him. We simply passed over him and he'd attacked. In any case, there was a second bump and I started looking around for a shark.

Then I spotted him, coming up ahead of us on our starboard quarter. I swung the sub around and he veered to our left, away from the wall. I banked the sub around trying to face him so Al could get some film footage. He suddenly rushed around us again in a complete circle of only fifteen feet radius. I continued to circle around and he went out of my field of vision. There was a third bump and I continued to circle. As I did so I saw this thing glinting in the sunlight and drifting downward like a leaf, sashaying back and forth as it sank. Then I realized it was a piece of the canopy. I turned around and I could see that, on the right hand side, by Al, the lower portion of the window was gone. I pointed to it. Al looked back and quickly stuck his tank there in case the bastard came back and made another attack. In any event the shark by this time had disappeared and we couldn't find him again. We cruised along and saw several more – they went through their usual displays but didn't attack and that was the last actual attack we had.

Since then I've seen a number of aggressive displays on the occasions that we've used the sub, but I haven't had a chance to do any more real shark-chasing with it. I went at several of them in the channel at Palau and produced the usual displays. Then out at Osprey Reef in the Coral Sea when we used it I got some displays and a couple of displays at the Marion reefs but in none of these was I close enough to provoke an attack and gain further observation.

At Eniwetok Attol, Ted Hobson (*Pacific Science*, 1963) conducted a series of fourteen experiments on the feeding behaviour of greys, blacktips, and whitetips. He concluded that for these sharks smell is the most effective sense for detecting prey, either injured or just in a state of stress, at a distance. Upcurrent they are able to follow such a stimulus to its source without the help of any other orienting stimuli. It releases a pattern of exploratory behaviour in grey sharks which promotes appetite. It takes some other specific stimulus to incite them highly. Despite the curiosity aroused by various stimuli, the approach to an unfamiliar situation is initially cautious but with increasing familiarity this caution will steadily subside.

With a motionless prey the grey's final phase of approach is normally directed by vision. Significant visual clues seem to involve the detection of movement, or contrasting brightness, or both. Visual acuity and the ability to distinguish form were not evident. In one experiment greys showed no preference between a four-inch cube of wood and a similar-sized cake of fish flesh. They accepted equally an intact fish or one with head and fins removed. But when offered the choice of a pair of three-inch fish cubes, one natural and one dyed black with nigrosine dye, in a total of 172 trials under all possible lighting conditions, the black was taken 124 times – seventy-two per cent of the total.

Further experiments showed that while grey sharks will initially accept baits such as fish flesh soaked in alcohol, such baits are promptly rejected when the taste is unacceptable.

In another experiment mollusc flesh such as that of the giant clam was paired with chunks of grouper flesh. The baits were taken with equal vigour, indicating a lack of visual discrimination, but the mollusc flesh was rejected almost immediately.

Tests with standard shark repellent copper acetate-nigrosine dye showed it to be ineffective when grey sharks were present in numbers and motivated by food adjacent to the repellent.

11

Great White Death

Valerie Taylor

Several years ago, with the help of my diary, I decided to write down much of the general knowledge that I had accumulated on the 'Great White Death'.

No doubt my observations and experiences will differ greatly from those of other people who have had the opportunity to study this shark at close range.

However, with very little to go on other than my own observations, I did the best that I could. Not being a scientist, or a professional writer, I am sure that readers with such experience will be able to point out many errors.

I have put into print, however, for better or worse, a collection of incidents and experiences which I hope make interesting reading and may teach people a little about the shark, whose reputation and numbers have suffered so drastically since the release of *Jaws*.

The sharks that I write about are real ones, some of them probably still living, off the South Australian coast. Peter Benchley's monster was the fabrication of an imaginative mind, although he did use the characteristics of the real white with amazing effectiveness.

This piece does not cover all our experiences with the 'Great White Death'. They would fill a whole book, but there is enough information to give a good overall picture of the sharks and of some of the people who work with them.

■

There is one shark which is the epitome of all man's fears. It is not common or easily found. It is known by many names. *Carcharodon carcharias*. Great White Death. Man-eater.

The Great White Death is the ultimate predator – a superbly designed eating machine. There is no other animal alive which has evolved to the same degree of perfection, essentially unchanged for millions of years.

Its main enemies are others of its kind and, of course, man. Today there are still remote corners of the world, like the cold waters off the South Australian coast, where the Great White Death patrols the ocean in an eternal search for food, as its ancestors have done for sixty million years.

When Matthew Flinders first charted this coast in 1802, he wrote of the hundreds of large sharks that he saw. Their numbers have been declining ever since. Vulnerable because of their fearlessness, they are becoming increasingly rare. To find a white shark today is an uncertain and expensive business. To find one in twenty years' time could be impossible.

We believe that great whites live in a certain territory, despite the generally held opinion that they are ocean roamers. When we seek great whites, we sail into places where we know they live. Dangerous Reef, 19 miles from Port Lincoln is such a place. South Neptune Island further out is another.

In these areas, few females are seen. Most of the sharks are males, 11 to 15 feet long. Females are found at Kangaroo Island, 100 miles away. There appear to be fewer of them, and, as is the case with most shark species, they are larger – 16 to 20 feet in length.

The largest, all females, are found at Streaky Bay 186 miles west of Dangerous Reef. These are rare giants measuring up to 20 feet and weighing well over 2,500 pounds. The world record great white was taken here in 1964 by a man named Alf Dean and, although only 15 feet long, it weighed 2,664 pounds.

Big-game fishermen have tried to beat this record and, while several have claimed that they hooked bigger fish, none have been landed.

There are no records available on sightings of really small whites. Where do the babies live? Small whites are not uncommon around the North American coast, but these are not babies. I have been able to find few scientific records of really small great whites anywhere. Even pregnant females are not common.

The only reference I could find on this was a report that a pregnant female with two foetuses was caught on a line near Kangaroo Island, South Australia. Little is known of their breeding habits, but one thing I am sure of; white sharks are slow breeders and probably live a long time, perhaps hundreds of years. Also, they continue to grow. The largest white shark on record, taken near Port Ferry, Victoria, supposedly measured 36½ feet, but there is some question as to the validity of this claim.

The Great White Death may be an ocean roamer as many experts suggest, and it is probably true in some cases, but our experiences suggest that it is mainly a creature with a defined territory.

I believe that, in the Dangerous Reef area, we have lured some of the same sharks, year after year. In January 1973, all but one of the sharks lured to our chartered boat, the *Temptation*, acted in a way that suggested that they had experienced the cages before. In the past, the sharks had repeatedly attacked the cages. On that occasion, they carefully looked them over, then moved away, concentrating on the baits around the stern of the boat.

Their attitude was disastrous for our film work. Ron was forced to return to his original 1965 method of filming sharks. This meant hanging his unguarded body from the duckboard and filming the marauders as they attacked the lures, only feet away.

White sharks have some interesting habits. To me, the most fascinating is that they raise their heads from the water to investigate the unusual. It is rather nerve-racking seeing a 13-foot great white carefully watching one's every move, with its head above water.

This unsharklike mannerism could have resulted from hunting warm-blooded creatures which live along the shore. South Australian fishermen tell stories of whites lifting half their bodies clear of the water to grab a sleeping seal from a rock. I see no reason to doubt them, for the sharks certainly do lift their bodies several feet from the water time and time again, reaching for baits pulled well above the surface.

It will not, however, rise from the water six inches to reach a vulnerable human kneeling on a duckboard. It will watch in a most intelligent way. I am not saying that the great white is more intelligent than any other shark, just that its behaviour is different.

Apart from its immense size and aggressive disposition, it is this behaviour that makes him so special. It is not just the best armed, it is also the oddest shark I have ever met.

Sometimes a shark would swim past the boat without seeming to take any notice, then surprise us all by sneaking back under the hull and grabbing a bait before we realized what was happening.

This never happened with a person, although we all spent a lot of time kneeling or lying at water level and were within easy reach. We were obviously not their normal prey.

Both Ron and I, when working with sharks, try by behaviour and dress to make sure that the shark can recognize us as something other than natural food. So far this has worked perfectly, but it is not a proven fact and cannot be recommended as a surefire safety precaution.

The closest call we ever had with a white happened one night about 11·30 when neither dress nor behaviour were recognizable. There were three sharks around the boat, coming in one after the other trying for the baits. We were working with Italian film director, Bruno Valatti. Bruno had been filming sharks feeding at night.

We had noticed in the past that the usually calm, controlled, daytime great white shark turned more aggressive after dark. Our three had performed well for the cameras and I was in the tiny cabin of the *Temptation* when Bruno yelled, 'Ron's in, Ron's in the water!'

Everything stopped. Everything. I knew that Ron could not survive. He would die, torn to pieces in the cold black southern ocean.

Here is what I wrote in my diary at the time: '18.1.72. Late last night, I nearly lost Ron. At 11:45 PM. he slipped from Rodney Fox's 20-foot fibreglass boat into the oil slick. There were three big sharks feeding on half a horse. Everyone was stilled with horror, almost like statues unable to move. The wind and current were carrying Rodney's boat away fast. It was very dark and rough. Ron swam after the small boat away from the baits and blood. He wore no diving equipment but being a strong swimmer reached Rodney's boat within 30 seconds and grasped the bow. He tried to pull himself from the water but lacked the strength. Hand over hand, he inched his way around the gunwhale, his body from the hips down still immersed. As Ron reached the stern, Rodney helped him up over the motors. Rodney said later Ron virtually flew into the boat. As his legs cleared the surface, a great grey shape loomed up beneath him and the big black eye watched for a second before moving under the stern.'

Ron had been helping Rodney anchor the cages away from the *Temptation*, and, while jumping from one boat to the other, had slipped on the oily deck.

The previous day, Ron had spared a white shark, now the favour had been returned. I was in the cage with Ron when it happened.

A beautiful big male, twelve feet long, had been performing well against the bars. Ron was shooting movie, and I, still photographs. Our rather skimpy cage was tethered to the *Temptation* by a slender steel trace which hung an inch or so below the water level.

The shark, which had been circling us about 4 feet down, suddenly came in on the surface. His nose touched the trace and, with a sudden start, the shark flicked back, twisting a loop of steel around his head. Frightened, he dived deep, found himself trapped, and went into a characteristic spin, binding the cable even more firmly around his body.

The cage plunged and bucked like a mad thing. I thought we would be killed. Ron was not using scuba. Fortunately for me, I was.

Sometimes, the cage would be under the water for a minute or more before the flotation tanks pulled us back to the surface, where Ron could grab a quick breath of air.

Not realizing how tangled it was, our friends on board cast the trace off, hoping that the shark would free himself. Our ride became wilder. The trapped shark twirled with incredible suppleness, twisting back, again and again, to bite the wire that held it.

The shark eventually began to tire. Although battered, I started taking stills. Ron, with his usual calmness, had been filming whenever possible. The above-water cameramen had stood and stared without shooting a single frame!

Once the shark became exhausted, it hung head down from the cage, giving only an occasional flutter. We then used Rodney's boat to tow the shark to shallow water in the lee of Dangerous Reef. Ron sat on a rock, and removed the trace from around the shark. The white's expressionless eye seemed to roll back, watching every move. Once the tail was free, Ron gave the shark a push and it swam out into deeper water, then turned in a big circle and returned to where Ron stood.

He pushed it once again toward the open sea. The great tail lashed the water once and, in a flurry of spray, the shark vanished. Only a surface swell marked its path. Ron spared the shark; the following night it was Ron that was spared.

The accidental capture of a white shark may appear a rarity, but almost exactly one year later, on 2 January 1973, it happened again in the same way. This time, to our amazement, the shark was a female, the first that any of us had ever seen in this area.

It is easy to determine the sex of a shark. Males have two large claspers situated between their anal fins. Females do not.

She hung a forlorn sight, completely exhausted from her struggles, her tail securely attached to the cage. Rodney, Ron, and I went into the water to take photographs.

The shark suffered us to crawl all over her. Only once did she break into a violent struggle, sending Rodney and I swimming frantically away while Ron dashed in, camera whirring.

All the while her eyes watched us. She was exhausted, but very much alive and aware of us.

We dragged her into shallow water, tail first. She had suffered severe bruising as the steel wires grated over her body. Anoxia was causing her to roll sickeningly. Once the waves started breaking over her, she recovered quickly and would have swum away but for the restricting coils of metal.

Ron and I were both in the water with her. We jabbed a metal name tag through her dorsal fin, making her the second great white we had tagged. It read: 'O'Gower. UNI. N.S.W. 2000 ... No.11.'

Professor Ken O'Gower is Australia's leading shark researcher and for many years had been tagging sharks to assist in the study of their migratory habits.

Another shark expert, American Thomas A. Lineaweaver III, had asked us to take a great white's temperature – if we ever had the chance. Ever since receiving this request, we had carried two large thermometers around, just in case.

This was the chance, Ron drove a slender knife six inches into the fleshy part of her back, near the spine. He then inserted a thermometer into the wound. The body temperature was 22.55°C. The water temperature was 20.5°C. It is believed that the muscle action of 'game fish' generates a certain amount of heat, but the shark had, by now, been virtually motionless for over three hours.

She was becoming anxious to go. I could feel her tail muscles swimming within themselves. A quick run over with a tape showed her to be 13 feet long – she was quite a big lump of shark.

We set her free. She hesitated for a second, then, with a sweep of her tail, flowed away from us for ever.

Six months later, Mr Peter E. Huggins, a professional shark fisherman from Colac, Victoria, caught our tagged shark. He returned the tag to Professor O'Gower with details as to how she died and how much a pound her flesh brought at the fish market.

One day, some qualified person may be interested enough to research whites in their natural element. I only hope when that day arrives there are enough great whites left to make the study worthwhile.

Whites are reasonably plentiful wherever there are large colonies of seagoing mammals. They may be found around harpooned whales, or attacking schools of fish, but they live near seal colonies.

The white shark acts as nature's culler, sorting out the sick, the old, and the feeble, leaving only the strong and healthy to perpetuate the species.

I have never seen seals chased from the water by a shark, but I have seen a shark chased by a young bull sea lion. This astounding incident occurred the afternoon of 1 January 1973.

A 13-foot shark had swum up the slick and was circling *Temptation*. To let him know he had found the right place, we threw out several baits. Once the shark arrives it is important to feed him, otherwise he could become bored and go away.

This shark had taken a bait and was beginning to perform well. Ron and I were about to enter the cages when a young bull sea lion swam out from the reef and began to annoy the shark.

It was really quite incredible. The seal would constantly leap through the surface, then dive at the shark. Although concentrating on the tail, the seal darted around the predator's head several times. He gave it no peace. There were seven people watching and we all agreed the bull seal appeared to be following or chasing the shark.

The white shark must have thought so too, because he became more agitated, swimming faster to annoy the seal. Finally, after 10 to 15 minutes, the shark swam away. We never saw him again.

I could hardly believe it. A 250-pound seal had harrassed a 1,200-pound shark into leaving the area. We had just spent five days and one thousand dollars enticing the shark to us. Now he was gone, and we had to start all over again.

The victorious young bull swam back to his island, lumbered up the rocks, and plopped down in the sun, where he promptly went to sleep. It appeared that playing with white sharks was all in a day's fun for him.

The most interesting piece of information to emerge from this incredible incident is that even a great white beginning to fall into a feeding pattern can be deterred. The shark had swum possibly 20 miles, or more, following the whale oil slick. On arrival, it must have been hungry and ready to eat, yet a bothersome little seal had forced it away. One would imagine a white shark tearing the mammal to pieces. We were all waiting for something like that to happen.

I had the feeling that what we witnessed was not an unusual happening, but a course of action used by the Australian sea lions. Ron and I discussed this event for some time, our main interest being that if a seal could harass a big shark like that, could similar behaviour by a diver produce the same result? In any and every case where a diver confronted a white shark with aggression, the shark eventually departed.

All the divers I know who've survived an attack by a great white say they never saw the shark before it hit them.

I am not saying that if a potential victim sees the shark before the attack he can frighten it away, just that it appears to be a great psychological advantage to show aggression. Sharks certainly seem to know when they are being watched or threatened. It is something they do not normally encounter in their day-to-day life.

Sharks also learn simple things quickly. There is obvious mistrust of the boat and its occupants. It is always a painstaking business to coax these sharks to feed. Once you do, it is interesting to watch how quickly their subconscious feeding behaviour takes over. Having another white feeding around the boat helps a lot. The shark's brain is impregnated by hereditary behaviour patterns over which the owner, once the signal is strong enough, has little control. Sharks can also think – and some better than others.

It would be interesting to know at what stage conscious thought is replaced by blind instinct. With whaler sharks this happens very quickly. In most whites, particularly ones who have experienced big-game fishermen, blind instinct seems always to be tempered by either conscious thought or subconscious fear.

In the Indian Ocean, we were filming hundreds of sharks feeding on a harpooned whale. I was kept busy beating them off with a short metal stick. Constantly aiming for the eyes, I must have landed hundreds of blows. Some persisted more than others. After I had jabbed them several times, I noticed an amazing thing. By shaking my stick at a previously hit shark from a distance of up to twenty feet, I could make that shark flinch, jam his gills tightly shut, roll his eye back, and flick away.

This happened with not just one shark, but many sharks. They were mainly oceanic whitetips, 8 to 10 feet long, though one oceanic blue performed in a somewhat similar manner. Within half an hour, these supposedly mindless man-eating predators had learned a simple lesson. If they bumped me, I bumped them back hard, and they did not like it!

I think that white sharks would behave under similar conditions in the same manner. Unfortunately, I will never be able to prove this theory properly, for whites do not bump before they bite. They just bite. Even a gentle nip from a great white is disastrous.

Whites appear to be very afraid of each other. If several sharks have been attracted at the same time, they take turns attacking the cages, never swimming in together. Should two sharks be on a collision course (and it does happen), each, on sighting the other, will flick away at great speed.

In *Blue Water, White Death* there appeared to be only one great white shark. In fact, there were five all around the boat at the same time. We could rarely film them together, because they did not swim together.

One white, several feet longer than the rest, appeared to have an unchallenged right of way. If it approached the bait at the same time as another, the smaller one always gave way immediately as they were in sight of each other.

I have never seen a white shark in a feeding frenzy. Whites take everything in a slow, calculated fashion. Even when fighting for a bait, the great jaws snapping, there is perhaps a sudden burst of energy, but no continued frenzy.

They are cannibals by nature and will attack a wounded comrade with the same impunity as they attack a box, a boat, or even, occasionally, man. Fortunately, man is not a food that they like. I believe most attacks have been mistakes.

At the time of this writing, there have been only thirteen positive deaths due to white shark attack recorded in Australia. Not a very impressive record for a shark, particularly when compared with the 140-odd attacks attributed to the bronze whaler, *Carcharhinus macrurus*, a smaller relative of the white shark.

On 12 March 1960, Brian Rodgers was attacked by a 9-foot white pointer (another name for the great white) during a spearfishing competition near Aldinga Beach, South Australia. Brian drove off the shark, made a tourniquet for his injured leg with speargun rubber, and swam towards the shore three-quarters of a mile away. He was picked up by divers in a boat and rushed to hospital where three hundred stitches were inserted in his torn leg.

Rodney Fox, who was fishing in the same area also saw the shark when it circled him several times. Rodney said he pointed his spear gun at the predator and felt as though he were pointing a match, the gun looked so small by comparison. The shark vanished leaving Rodney shaken but unharmed.

Two years later, on 10 December 1962, during another spear-fishing competition, sixteen-year-old Geoffrey Corner met a shark just 14 miles from where Brian had been attacked. Geoffrey's spearfishing competitor, Allen Phillips, dragged the mutilated boy from the shark's maw, but he was dead before reaching the beach.

Exactly one year to the day after Geoffrey's death, Rodney Fox was fishing in the South Australian spearfishing championships, one hundred yards from where Brian Rodgers was attacked. This time Rodney was not so lucky. He did not see the shark until it had his body crushed in its mouth.

Although critically wounded, Rodney fought his way free and was picked up by a nearby safety boat. Rodney survived, where most would have died. His ribs were crushed, his lungs punctured and his liver torn. Only Rodney's physical and mental fitness pulled him through. Rodney decided he was going to live and, although all the odds were against him, he did.

There is a strong possibility that Brian, Rodney and Geoffrey were all attacked by the same beast. Perhaps the shark was merely trying to deter intruders from its territory or was it a mad ravenous brute trying to kill anything that crossed its path? Unfortunately, the answer is something we will never know.

The last of our friends to be attacked by a great white was Henri Bource. Henri had his leg bitten off at the knee while he was swimming with a group of sea lions. The shark was dragging Henri down by his leg when the shark teeth severed the bone at the knee. As Henri was not using scuba, he is extremely lucky not to have drowned. When the attack occurred, he was not the only diver in the water. His companions beat back the shark with hand spears as it followed Henri to the boat.

In each of these cases, there were other people in the water when the attacks took place. Was it just bad luck or were they the particular victims singled out for some reason? Certainly, carrying bleeding fish on the weight belt increases the chances of attracting a shark.

It is very much to their credit that they are back diving again.

Many years of experience have proved to my satisfaction that sharks do not attack without a reason. Either the victim has unwittingly done something to attract the shark or, as in the case of Raymond Short, who was bitten in shallow water near Sydney, the shark was sick and wounded.

The few whites that I have met accidentally have shown a certain curiosity, but no inclination to attack. They have simply flashed past, looked us over, returned for a second look, then disappeared. Had we been spearing fish and the sharks hungry, things may have happened differently.

When a shark's feeding instinct is aroused, they are likely to attack and try to devour anything from a beer can to a 60-foot boat. If animal blood is poured into the water near white sharks, they will swim through the red cloud, jaws snapping with tremendous ferocity. They appear to be feeling with their teeth for the owner of the blood and will usually bite, viciously, the first solid object to cross their path.

Ron and I have prolonged experience only with white sharks which we have lured with food. They are so rarely seen otherwise, it is difficult to guess what the pattern of their everyday lives is. Food would be the main interest, but, beyond that, little is known about them.

Unfortunately, whites do not take kindly to being trapped in tanks and generally die before any extensive research can be done. The only white I know of kept in captivity constantly bumped the walls of his tank. In nature, they know no restrictions, in captivity they refuse to accept them.

An unexpected feature of the great white is that it does not have to be in motion to breathe. Both of our trapped sharks managed perfectly well hanging motionless, by their tails, for several hours.

A great white is easy to recognise under water, the most distinctive feature being his round black eye. Unlike other members of his particular family, his serrated triangular teeth are always showing in a sinister smile. The tail is also very distinctive. Most sharks have a tail with the top lobe much longer than the bottom. The great white has a tail with lobes of almost equal length, a modification shared by several other fast-moving sharks and most big pelagic fish.

One trait all sharks have in common is that they can be very unpredictable, and it is this unpredictability that makes them potentially dangerous.

The contrast in behaviour between whites and whalers will show what I mean. We had five male whites of roughly equal size and weight swimming around our boat. After a short time, we knew each individually. There was a definite pecking order.

The leader was more aggressive and had the right of way. He took more baits and approached the boat more frequently. Another similar shark circled further away from the boat and took no baits at all. It was hungry or it wouldn't have been there, yet it was timid and appeared to be easily bullied by the others. According to Professor O'Gower, this is not uncommon behaviour in some species.

On the other hand the whalers have little or no respect for their leader, at least during feeding. A group of various-sized whaler sharks will attack lures in a mad, mixed-up scramble.

This type of behaviour could be the reason white sharks have made so few attacks on man and whalers so many.

Looking at all the records available to me on whites, I discovered a confusing number of theories but little fact. Considering that the Great White Death is the most awesome predator living on earth today, this is rather surprising. Scientists may or may not agree with what I have written here, but the majority of my statements are based on personal experience and the rest on the experiences of personal friends.

III Scientific

The segment from Dr Eugenie Clark's book, *The Lady and the Sharks*, is titled 'Sharks that Ring Bells.' It is the only completely scientific experiment concerning sharks that I found suitable for inclusion. In fact, there is very little data available on experiments concerning sharks and their behaviour that makes good general reading. The result is that Dr Clark has a section all her own.

True, I could have included 'Sharks that Ring Bells' in the shark behaviour section, but it hardly seemed the correct thing to do. The other stories under 'Shark Behaviour' are mostly odd little snippets about a shark or sharks that came to the author's attention for some special reason regarding their actions at the time. My story about grey nurses came about because we were trying to make a film, not do scientific research into their behaviour.

Most of the other scientific books I considered, while not uninteresting to me, concentrated more on describing sharks and where they could be found. For instance, 'Leopard Shark, *Triakis semifasciata,* shallow water, eastern north Pacific, five gill slits' and so on. This type of information, while useful to someone who wants to know all the particulars about a certain shark, hardly makes good reading for the general public.

Anyway, Dr Eugenie Clark is such an unusual person and her work so important to the understanding of sharks, I feel she deserves a special place of her own in this book.

12

'Sharks that Ring Bells'
From *The Lady and the Sharks*

Eugenie Clark

Eugenie Clark is a remarkable woman. She was the founder and director, for the first ten years of its existence, of the Cape Haze Marine Laboratory in Florida.

During her period with the lab, it evolved from a tiny, one-woman affair based in a 20 by 12 foot wooden building into one of the most respected institutions of its type in the world.

I have had the pleasure of meeting Dr Clark many times, mainly when working together on the adventure cruise ship *Lindblad Explorer*. She has the inquisitive mind of a good scientist and her research into sharks and their behaviour patterns has done much to further man's limited knowledge of these large fish.

The first book of Dr Clark's that I read was called *Lady with a Spear*. It was enjoyable reading and I found it encouraging that this world-famous marine scientist regarded marine animals not just as objects of research, but as living, feeling, thinking creatures, each with its own personality. *The Lady and the Sharks* is even better. It is full of interesting facts and information presented in an exciting easy-to-read style.

The chapter I have chosen tells how foolish people can be about sharks. Had the four-year-old child dangling its legs in the shark pen been bitten, all blame would, no doubt, have fallen on the shark and Eugenie Clark. The parents ignored No Trespassing signs and crossed a chained-off driveway, but would have aimed their outrage and sorrow at the shark rather than themselves.

The experiments with the lemon sharks ringing bells is fascinating, as is the description of sharks copulating. I am often asked how sharks mate. This is the only time that I have ever read of someone actually watching and recording the event in such fine detail.

Most famous of the experiments, and one which is quoted in other subsequent books on sharks, is that concerned with the training of sharks to ring a bell for food. It may not seem like a very significant or useful achievement, but, prior to this, it was generally believed that sharks had very limited intelligence and could not be trained to do anything. This programme proved that they can not only be trained but that they learn fairly quickly.

The same basic programme was later extended to test the visual perceptions of sharks. A number of interesting things came out of this – including the fact that some species of sharks are very attracted to strong striped patterns, information that should be passed on to the swimwear designers, and perhaps, Dr Walter Starck, inventor of the banded wetsuit.

In a later chapter, she calls a special shark friendly. I know that they can be friendly, but generally hate to say it. After *Jaws* most people think nothing nice about sharks, least of all that they can be friendly.

I would like every person who has seen and been frightened by *Jaws* to read Dr Clark's book for a balanced picture of sharks as they really are. A better book would be hard to find, for it is a warm, quite funny account of an interesting woman in love with the sea.

■

As the lab became better known, the problem of unwelcome visitors arose. Once we found an 11-foot tiger shark dead in our pen with the hook of a large, long-handled dip net jammed over its gills. This was a particularly handsome shark that was living well in our pen and eating huge quantities of shark meat left over from our routine dissections. We couldn't imagine how the naked wire hoop of the dip net, which Beryl had left on the dock until he had time to put a new net on it, got into the pen and over the shark's head. Beryl learned how when he was getting a haircut. The man in the next chair was telling his barber.

'That Cape Haze Marine Lab is a dangerous place,' he said, and went on to tell how he and his wife went down to look around one day, but nobody was there and the buildings were locked up. They were fascinated by the large tiger shark in the pen and, finding the big hoop with the long handle decided to see if they could make the shark swim through the hoop. As the shark swam close to the dock, the man's wife held on to the end of the eight-foot handle and lowered the hoop directly in the shark's path. The shark swam into it, but the pectoral fins prevented the hoop from getting further than the gill region. 'That goddam shark was ready to pull my wife into the water if she hadn't let go the handle,' he told the barber. They then hurried away from the 'dangerous' lab, leaving the tiger shark to thrash itself to death.

Beryl and I decided we had to take more precautions, and as much as we disliked putting up eyesores, we made No Trespassing signs and put a chain across the driveway to the lab. This discouraged most off-hour visitors, but not the worst kind. As the lab grew, we had to put up stronger warning signs and barbed-wire fencing. Even then, I sometimes caught trespassers in the act when I was working late at the lab or on a Sunday. One Sunday, I looked up from my desk and was horrified to see a child about four years old sitting on the feeding platform dangling his feet in the shark pen. His parents had brought him. They had ignored the signs and climbed the fence. They saw no sharks in the pen and were wandering around the grounds. An 11-foot dusky shark was swimming in the deeper murky water of the pen. Fortunately it had eaten its fill the day before.

One evening, when I had to work very late, I watched as a man, pushing down one barbed wire with his foot and lifting the upper wire with his hand, allowed a pretty girl to step through. I caught up with them as they neared the shark pen and he was saying, 'Wait till you see this!' I interrupted their adventure and talked with them. He defiantly told me, 'We weren't going to harm your precious sharks,' I might have lost my temper except I was stalling for time. I had already called the police.

The couple was arrested. The arrest, announced in the paper the next day, was enough to keep trespassers away for some time.

Another time, a man with three young ladies in his boat pulled up alongside a small pen which held twenty baby sharks we had delivered the day before and were hoping would live. The man began showing off by catching one of the two-foot sharks by the tail, twirling it around his head, and hurling it across the pen while his audience giggled. He quickly started up his motor when he saw me coming out of the lab.

We continued setting out lines for sharks. After a day of diving on the reefs, Beryl would check the shark line on the way back and we might return to the lab with garbage cans of two-inch gobies, blennies, and serranids and a twelve-foot shark. I kept on experimenting and studying abdominal pores and anything else I could learn about the sharks we caught. This led to a series of experiments that ultimately got too much publicity and stuck me with the dubious label of 'shark lady'.

Somehow my reputation of diving and using a spear to collect fishes (described in my book *Lady with a Spear*) made reporters and writers of magazine articles assume that I collected big sharks by diving and spearing them. Even when I corrected this notion in an interview and stipulated before the interview that I be allowed to see the text of the article before it was sent to press (something popular-magazine writers and editors hate to do), many bloopers got through. In one case, the writer carefully avoided any hint that I dived with and speared the sharks I worked with, but when the art department of the magazine got to work, they sketched a picture of me diving, with a one-rubber arbalete spear gun that would barely hold a mullet, about to shoot the spear into a gigantic shark. This came out as a two-page spread in the magazine.

The things we were learning about sharks and our success in keeping sharks in captivity drew the attention of scientists from various parts of the world who were interested in problems related to sharks. They came from Africa, Germany, Italy, Israel, England, France, Denmark, and Japan to work with us. We were able to expand our research with additional financial help we got in the form of grants from the National Science Foundation, the Office of Naval Research, the American Philosophical Society, and the Selby Foundation.

There are about 250 different species of sharks living in the world, ranging from a cute little deep-water species less than a foot long to the giant whale shark reported to attain 60 feet in length. The largest shark that ever lived was *Carcharodon megalodon*. Its black and grey fossilized teeth, measuring up to six inches, are commonly found on Florida beaches. It probably grew to nearly 100 feet in length and is related to the most dangerous man-eating shark now living, the great white shark, *Carcharodon carcharias*. Fortunately, the white shark grows to only 20 feet.

The wide shallow continental shelf extending about 100 miles out on the west coast of Florida limits the variety of sharks we can catch to about eighteen species. For practical reasons, we had to operate our shark lines within eight miles of shore and had little chance of catching real deep-water or oceanic sharks. We caught three different species of hammerhead sharks, two species of blackfin sharks, several types of small dogfish sharks, and on rare occasions a white shark or a sand tiger shark. But we could count on a good supply of dusky and sandbar sharks each winter, nurse sharks and tiger sharks all year round, and many bull and lemon sharks during the spring, summer, and fall.

Most of the sharks we caught were from 5 to 11 feet long. We measured a few dusky, tiger, and great hammerhead sharks that got into the 12- and 14-foot range and nearly 1,000 pounds, but this size group is uncommon in our records.

Our examinations of the contents of hundreds of sharks' stomachs showed us that our local sharks eat over forty varieties of fish, including eels, some prickly bony fishes (e.g., spiny blowfish and poisonous spined catfish), stingrays, and other sharks. We also often found remains of squid, octopus, shellfish, starfish, crabs, and shrimps, occasionally sea turtles and sea birds, and rarely some porpoise remains. Once we found a yellow-bellied cuckoo and another time a gull with a metal band (which was reported to the amazed bander) in the stomach of the omnivorous tiger shark.

Most of the species we studied seem to mate in the spring and early summer. At this time, the claspers of mature males were red and swollen. Often sperm oozed out of the urogenital papilla,* and on dissection we could see the testes were much enlarged. When we opened the female, we could find wriggling sperm by examining under the microscope smears taken from the vagina, uterus, and tubes leading toward the ovary. On the ovary, large yellow ripe round eggs were nearly ready to break out of their follicles. Shortly after the mating season, the ovary would contain only small white eggs, but the uterus would contain big yellow oval-shaped eggs. These had been fertilized by sperm at some point high in the tubes, and partway down the tubes in the nidamental or shell gland had acquired a soft golden 'shell' before settling into spongy pickets in the uterus. Sometimes we found each oval egg had a tiny wriggling embryo on the surface of the yolk.

By plotting the size of these embryos at different months of the year, we could draw their growth curve and determine the gestation period, which varied from eight to fourteen months, depending on the species. The females of most species we studied seem to have a litter of pups only once in two or three years.

The size of the litter depends to some extent on the species of shark. The sand tiger shark has only two young at a time, and these, according to Stew Springer, start feeding before they are born on eggs the mother continues to supply from the ovary. The bull, dusky, sandbar, and lemon sharks have from five to seventeen young at a time; the great hammerhead can have several dozen, and the tiger shark over a hundred. The older the mother shark gets, the greater the number of young she carries when pregnant. We also observed a few 'senile' big sharks whose ovaries had apparently stopped functioning.

Our shark dissections, especially on pregnant females, supplied fascinating information on the reproductive habits of some large species of sharks about which little was known previously. The most interesting part of our work with sharks was studying the live animal, working with one individual day after day for long periods of time and getting to know its personality.

One of the most extraordinary sharks I ever got to know was one I gave up for dead the day we caught her in May 1958. She was an adult lemon shark nearly 9 feet long. This was before we devised better methods for bringing live sharks from our setlines in the gulf back to the lab. We towed this shark by the hook she had taken in her mouth and firmly set in her jaw. It was a rough day. She was bounced on large waves in the gulf, and once we got her in the bay, we had to

---

* During copulation, sperm from the urogenital papilla enters a groove in the clasper, which swings into a forward position and is inserted into the female.

drag her across shallow barnacle flats because of the low tide. All the time, her mouth was being held open by the hook and towline, and water poured into her.

She struggled weakly when we first found her caught on the line. By the time we had her in the large fish pen alongside the lab's dock, she appeared dead. We tried to revive her by 'walking' her around the shallow end of the pen – pushing and pulling her gently so that the water would flow over her gills – but she didn't respond.

We finally gave up. It was too late in the day to hoist her onto the dock to weigh, measure, and dissect her. So we tied her limp form alongside the dock, still with the hook and setline in her mouth, and left, intending to work on her in the morning.

When we saw her next, she was a very lively shark, raising a commotion at the end of the dock. We put her into the pen again, in shallow water where she could not struggle too much. We held her down, propped her mouth open with a block of wood, and removed the hook. We had to cut the hook wound open a little wider, in order to back out the barbed hook with long-handled pliers. As soon as we released her, she swam vigorously around the pen and then slowed down to an effortless glide. Only gentle undulating movements of the end of her body and tail were needed to propel her powerful, streamlined body.

So we began to learn how hardy lemon sharks are, unlike other active sharks, and how well they can adjust to captivity. In the years that followed, we found it easy to bring lemon sharks in from our lines in good condition.

After the shark had spent a day in captivity, we discovered the probable reason for her weakness on the line – seven newborn lemon sharks, each about two feet long, swimming with her in the pen.

It was the first time a shark had given birth naturally at the lab. We had removed many living embryos and near full-term pups from gravid dusky and sandbar female sharks we dissected. Those babies, even when we tried 'incubator' methods, seldom lived more than a few days. But we had great hopes for raising the newborn lemon sharks.

The day after they were born, they started feeding. The female and her pups had our large 40 by 70-foot pen all to themselves. In a few weeks, they were eating well and the babies grew noticeably fatter. The sight of a person walking to the corner of the shallow end of the pen, where the young sharks were fed, attracted them almost immediately, and the first piece of cut fish dropped into the water set up a feeding frenzy as the seven young sharks crisscrossed each other and rushed around the feeding area.

Then I made a mistake. Our setlines caught a large male lemon shark, and I thought he would make a good mate for the female. We put him in the pen and he did get along fine with her. But the baby sharks began disappearing one by one. Those healthy young sharks, which would have been ideal for testing the function of abdominal pores because of their small size, were soon all gone.

We were left, however, with a handsome pair of adult lemon sharks that were very responsive to signs of food. We had an excellent opportunity to study their feeding behaviour.

At first we threw fish (whole mullet) to them. We used so much mullet to bait our shark lines and to feed the sharks we kept alive that we invested in a storage freezer. It paid for itself with the money we saved buying mullet wholesale, 200 pounds at a time.

In order to watch more closely when the sharks were feeding, we built a feeding platform close to the water. We weighed the amount of food we gave them each day, since I found out that practically nothing was known about the amount of food needed to keep a large shark alive. We could make the sharks come to the edge of the platform and take mullet handed to them. Occasionally a shark would miss and a mullet dropped to the bottom, especially when the shark charged toward the platform with open mouth and the feeder understandably let go of the mullet a fraction of a second early. Then we couldn't be sure which shark got the food.

A bright junior high school student, Tommy Romans, was a regular visitor to our lab and begged us to let him be a volunteer-worker and, among other things, to let him feed the sharks. The risk we ran having an 'attractive hazard' was unavoidable for our studies, but we could avoid letting a fourteen-year-old boy feed sharks from a platform suspended over the pen. Tommy was very persuasive. It could have been annoying except that he was so pleasant. He started working for us, helping in the weighing, measuring, and dissection of dead sharks. He also looked around for any odd jobs he could do, was quick to grab the hose and scrub down the dock when a dissection was over, sweep out the lab floors, wash our aquariums, empty garbage, help bait hooks on the boat – always showing almost the same enthusiasm and willingness to do these jobs as to join us skin diving. He was a fine diver and loved helping collect small fishes and putting up the shark line, especially when something was tugging on it. He fed all the little gobies, blennies, serranids, and other animals in the aquarium room, and soon took over weighing and preparing the food for the big sharks.

He watched us feed the sharks. One shark, making a clumsy pass at a mullet, bumped into the feeding platform which at high tide was at water level. (When the tide was extra high, we didn't feed the sharks. A foot could be mistaken for a mullet.) The mullet fell down, and both sharks went after it. The sharks never fought over the food, but even their gentlest movements around the feeding platform stirred up the soft muck on the bottom of the pen, and you could see down only 2 or 3 feet of the 7-foot depth. We couldn't tell which of the two sharks had got the mullet. Also, we now had a big nurse shark in the pen which stayed on the bottom most of the time.

'Why don't we tie a weak string on the mullet until the shark takes it?' suggested Tommy. It was a good idea, and Tommy undertook the task of tying each mullet with a string several feet long and wrapping the length neatly around the fish, so that it could be thrown to the shark like confetti and the strings wouldn't tangle in the bucket of fish. The sharks came quickly to the splash at the surface, and the mullet could then be pulled into a convenient position for camera studies before a shark was allowed to take the food. This method took away the hazard of feeding the sharks by hand; the records of food consumed by each shark became more accurate and Tommy had won himself the job of feeding them. His interest went deeper. He began borrowing books from our library to take home. And would discuss them with me the next day. I wondered if he was ever getting his regular school homework done.

Dr Lester Aronson, an expert in animal psychology, came to the lab during the early summer of 1958. 'Has anyone ever made a study of the learning behaviour of sharks?' I asked him.

Dr Aronson told us that some experiments on the olfactory sense of small sharks had been done. Plugging a nostril will cause a dogfish to swim in circles toward the unplugged side if a scent of food is in the water. But no sophisticated experiments of the kind done with birds and rats had been tried on sharks. Sharks, being such primitive fish with a primitive brain and poorly developed visual apparatus, were generally considered rather stupid – poor subjects for the classical experiments done with higher animals. 'Besides', he said 'they're difficult to keep as experimental animals, and no one has tried putting them into a Skinner box!'

'Our sharks are smart, and, boy, can they see us coming, with the food!' Tommy said defending his pets.

Dr Aronson then encouraged us. 'You certainly have a unique and good setup for testing their ability to learn some simple task.'

We prompted Dr Aronson further and before the day was over we had a plan. He suggested that we place a target in the water and train the shark to take mullet from the target in such a way that the shark would bump its nose against it, which would ring a bell. After a long training period, we conditioned a shark to associate the target with food, and to press the target and ring the bell even when the food was no longer presented along with the target.

Before he returned to New York, Dr Aronson helped us work out a design for the apparatus to try an experiment in 'instrumental conditioning,' using the feeding end of the shark pens as a kind of Skinner box.

'I wish I could stay longer and help try to train those sharks. They do look smart. Don't be discouraged. It may take months, but it really will be something if you can succeed.'

At the end of the summer, Tommy hated to leave the lab. Oley Farver, another ex-commercial fisherman, had started working with us. Oley, with Tommy's assistance, had built a longer, stronger, platform with a railing. He also built a special arm to which the target, a 16 by 16-inch plywood square painted white, could be attached during feeding tests. The target could be placed so that it was just below the water surface regardless of the tide, and a firm push on it would close an electrical circuit, causing a submerged bell (an ordinary six-volt doorbell sealed in a metal cylinder) to ring.

Near the end of September, we started a strict training programme for the sharks. Every day at 3·00 P.M., Oley and I put the target in the water a maximum of 20 minutes and fed the sharks in front of it, dangling the mullet from a string. At first the sharks seemed wary of the target and hesitated to take the food. But after a few days they could be lured in so close that in order to get the food into its mouth, each shark was forced to press its nose against the target. We increased the intensity of the bell from a weak buzz the first week to a loud ring that could be heard clearly above the water by the end of the second week.

From our feeding records, we were surprised to learn that it took only 15 pounds of mullet a week to keep a full-grown lemon shark of nine feet healthy and active. If we gave them all they could eat, each would take more than 30 pounds at one time, but then they fed poorly or refused food for days. A shark in its natural habitat probably goes weeks, or even months during cold weather, without eating and then may find a huge meal, such as a weakened porpoise or sea turtle, that will keep it going for another long period without food.

In order to keep our lemon sharks in training every day, and to make them repeat pressing the target and ringing the bell as many times as possible each day, we cut the mullet into smaller and smaller pieces until each shark had to ring the bell about six to ten times to get his daily quota of two pounds.

In a few weeks, the sharks were taking food from the target so rapidly that the daily training test was often over in less than 6 minutes. We had to devise a fast way to reload food on the target, for when one shark removed the food the other shark was often directly behind. We attached a thin wire to the centre of the target. To each piece of food we then attached a short loop of weak string. We looped all the pieces of food on the end of the wire that reached the platform.

As a shark pressed the target and removed the food, the next piece could be released to slide down the wire and be in place on the target as the second shark came.

We could see clearly how wrong was the old belief that a shark has to roll over to take a bite. Even though the mouth is on the underside of its head, the lemon sharks had no difficulty coming squarely at the target and removing the food without rolling. The snout projecting forward over the mouth, however, did make it necessary for the end of the snout to give the target a good bump in the process.

The large nurse shark we also had in the pen occasionally gummed up the training period. It wasn't satisfied with the food we gave it in another part of the pen. It wanted to get in on the act. But the nurse shark, *Ginglymostoma cirratum,* is quite different from the lemon shark, *Negaprion brevivostris.* It belongs to another family of awkward-looking sharks and is slower, more sluggish, and clumsy; it spends most of its time lying on the bottom, often under ledges or in dark caves. The adults are about the same size as lemon sharks (9 feet) but they have tiny eyes with much poorer vision. Our later tests on baby nurse sharks proved they have good vision. But the large nurse shark in the pen with the swift-feeding lemon sharks didn't seem to be able to see the target. Slowly it would pick up the scent of food and, unlike the lemons, could dangle in front of the target in a vertical position, holding this position by waving its broad fanlike pectoral (arm) fins while passing its small-toothed, blubber-lipped mouth over the surface of the target. It would smell and feel its way to the food with the help of its barbels, a pair of whiskers on either side of its mouth, and then, by closing its gill slits and opening its mouth, create a vacuum that would suck in the food and break the string, stealing the lemon shark's food without ringing the bell. The nurse shark got in the way so much that sometimes we'd have to poke him on the nose with a stick to get him away from the target so we could get on with the training of the lemons.

Afer six weeks of feeding the lemon sharks from the target, we gave them the big test. We put the target in the water at the appointed time but with no food on it. The male lemon shark who usually responded first rushed at the target with his mouth open, then swerved aside when he reached it and found no food. The second time, and for eight more times, he came in slowly, looking over the target without touching it, a few times brushing it lightly. Finally, he nuzzled the empty target hard enough to set off the automatic bell, and we quickly tossed out a reward piece of food wrapped in confetti string that hit the water with a splash just to the left of the target. The shark quickly grabbed the food, cutting the string with his teeth. In this first critical test period, he proved he had associated pressing the target with getting his food – by repeatedly pushing the empty target and then taking the food tossed to him.

The more timid female lemon shark took longer to respond to the empty target, but within three days both were working the target without hesitation. We had succeeded in 'instrumentally conditioning' the lemon sharks. The nurse shark gradually gave up.

We came to know the sharks as individuals. Even though they looked identical from above (except for markers we put on their dorsal fins), it was easy to tell which was the male and which was the female by the manner in which they swam, turned, and reacted to the target. The male was bolder, and often when he saw us bringing the target onto the platform, he would cut short his wide-circling swim around the pen, go to a position opposite the platform, and, as the target was being lowered into the water, swim directly at it and push it with force almost the instant it was under water.

The female would hold back until the male had gotten several pieces of food and satisfied his initial hunger before she would alternate working the target with him. She would approach the target from her wide-swimming circle and often press it gently with the side of her head, just barely enough to ring the bell.

We started dropping the reward food farther and farther away from the target, giving the sharks only 10 seconds to get the food after the bell sounded. This was to test their ability to learn to make a correct turn.

For some odd reason, probably having nothing to do with Coriolis force (the effect of the earth's rotation which causes a deflection to the right in the Northern Hemisphere and to the left in the Southern Hemisphere),* the sharks in our pens almost always swam in clockwise circles. After pressing the target, the shark would have to make a counterclockwise turn to be in the direction where the reward food splashed down. They were slow to break their swimming habit.

Usually a shark would press the target, make a clockwise circle, and come back for the food; however, with a time limit of 10 seconds, as we moved the food farther away, they had less chance to reach the food on a clockwise turn than on a counterclockwise turn. After a few long clockwise turns and reaching the food just as the 10 seconds were up and the food was being pulled out of the water, the sharks learned to make the counterclockwise turn.

And they learned something else we didn't anticipate. It was a

---

* I was somewhat startled when Dr Lochner, an acoustician working with sharks in South Africa, came to visit the lab and remarked that all the sharks (in his lab's tank) swim in counterclockwise direction. Just a coincidence, probably. The local sea-bottom topography and currents undoubtedly influence a shark's swimming pattern more than the earth's rotation.

dramatic sight for visitors to watch us lower the target into the water, have the shark rush to push the target, make a left turn, then swim 8 feet down the side of the pen and catch the food dropped there as it hit the water. Of course, this is an easy trick to teach a porpoise or a seal, mammals with intelligence on the level of a dog; but for the lowly shark – which some taxonomists consider so beneath the bony fishes in evolutionary development that they won't even classify it as a fish – this was an accomplishment.

I decided to make it more dramatic by training them to take a fast swim way down to the end of the 70-foot pen for their reward food each time they pressed the target. It would also be a good movie sequence for the film record I was trying to make. But as the food was tossed out farther and farther away from the target, it was the female who caught on first that when the bell rang she could get the food faster than the male if she just kept circling the food area instead of going to press the target. When the male pressed the target, the female took his food. Both sharks quickly learned that the one who pressed the target had the least chance of getting the food. They started to hold back from pressing the target, and I had to move the feeding place back nearer the target to continue the experiments.

We made a crude test of an acoustical factor. The sound of the bell cued off the feeder that the shark had pushed the target and the reward food could be tossed out. We suspected that the sharks heard the bell and that its sound had reinforced their learning. What would they do if they pushed the target and the bell didn't ring? One day, when everything had been running smoothly for some days and the sharks were building up excellent scores in our record book, we didn't use the bell.

As usual, the male charged the target immediately and hit it. No bell sounded but we dropped the reward food. The shark turned counterclockwise but slowed down, and then instead of going to the feeding area, he returned to the target. The next time he pushed the target, and for the rest of the test period, it didn't bother him that the bell didn't ring. He pushed the target and went for his food which Sam Hinton says should be called the Nobell Prize.

We continued to run the tests for eight weeks until, just before Christmas, the water temperature dropped below 70° F, and the sharks lost interest in eating and in pressing the target. Then we learned something about their winter 'hibernation' and memory.

The water temperature in the pens didn't go up to the seventies again until near the end of February, and the sharks started showing some interest in food again. All during the ten cold weeks, we had tried feeding them every few days with food on a string. On 19 February, we put the target in the water and the two lemon sharks pressed it as though there had never been an interruption in their daily routine with the target. We continued feeding the sharks by making them ring the bell, preparing them for more complex tests.

Dr Dugald Brown, chairman of the department of biology at the University of Michigan, came to do some experiments at the lab in late April. He was making some complicated physiological tests on isolated pieces of living tissue from a shark's heart, which he kept alive in a high-pressure tube in a saline solution bath. Sometimes he had to check this tissue at odd times. On the night of 1 May, near midnight, Dr Brown went to the lab to check the temperature of the bath containing the muscle tissue. After that, he walked out on the dock with a floodlight to see what the lemon sharks were doing. They were copulating.

The copulation of large sharks has never been witnessed before or since, that I know of. Only small species of relatively slow-moving sharks (like the California horned shark or the European dogfish) have been seen *in copula* – the male partly coiled around the female as they mate while resting on the bottom of an aquarium.

A male shark can easily be told from a female, even in young embryos, by paired modified extensions of their pelvic fins. These sizable claspers are possessed by the males of sharks, rays, sawfishes, and skates, all of which have internal fertilization. During copulation, one of the two pennonlike claspers is rotated into a forward position, inserted into the vagina of the female, and then the unusual head of the clasper is opened as a person might expand one's hand from a fist. Cartilaginous ridges and hooklike spurs form a complex pattern which differs and is characteristic for each species of shark. An experienced shark anatomist can often tell the species of shark by examining just a clasper, the way Dr Ron Rosen, the gonopodium expert on xiphophorin fishes, can tell the species of platyfishes and swordtails apart by just the structural pattern of the male's intromittent organ, part of the anal fin of these aquarium fishes.

Dr Brown couldn't make out any details from the dock, but he drew a sketch of the lemon sharks *in copula*. 'They kept right on swimming in wide circles around the pen. I watched them for one hour.'

The sharks were mating side by side, heads slightly apart but the posterior half of their bodies in such close contact and the swimming movements so perfectly synchronized that they gave the appearance of a single individual, a two-headed monster.

The next night, I stayed up with cameras and floodlights ready for use, and for the next week I drafted all reliable friends I could to help take watches through the night, but the sharks did not copulate again. Once, at dusk, the male lemon shark swam unusually close to the female and then sank, frozen in a curled position, to the bottom of the shallow end of the pen for four minutes. The claspers were noticeably pulled to the left side and appeared enlarged and slightly pink. A remora that usually accompanied the female shark was attached to the clasper region of the male shark with its sucking disc. We wondered if some seminal secretion was being released by the male lemon shark and acting as an attractant.

The female paid no special attention to the male during his stops, but occasionally she would stop her swimming and rest alongside the male. Once they both stopped swimming and rested side by side for twenty minutes. Actually, it may be more work for a lemon shark to stop swimming than to swim in slow circles. While swimming, a lemon shark keeps its mouth slightly open, and water passes in and is flushed over the gills and out of the five pairs of passive gill openings. The sphincter around the esophagus at the back of the shark's throat is held in a contracted position so water doesn't flow down into the stomach. The esophageal sphincter muscle probably gets tired and opens when a shark, worn out from fighting a hook and line, is towed behind a boat and water is forced down its throat. Very little muscular activity of the shark's body is needed to keep its streamlined body in motion. But when a shark stops swimming, it has to pump water over its gills to keep up an oxygen supply. The muscular apparatus to keep this pump system going and opening and closing the mouth and gills slits looks as if it uses more calories than are needed to keep up a leisurely swim.

All during May, the pair of lemon sharks seemed unusually close and, we imagined, affectionate. They often swam together side by side or in tandem for long periods. Although they ate a little less food at this time, they worked the target very well, and we conducted many kinds of experiments with them, especially on their swimming pattern and ability to hear sounds.

Then unwittingly I made a decision with tragic consequences. I had read in books that since no cones had been found in histological preparations of the shark retina, sharks were colour-blind. The retinal rods and a reflecting layer of guanin crystals at the back of a shark's eye were thought to be responsible for the shark's visual acuity in dim light and at night. And sharks seem more darkly poetic if you think of them as crepuscular creatures.

Just for fun, I decided to try a small test of our sharks' colour blindness. I painted the white target yellow. I figured the sharks would not notice the difference.

The male lemon shark lined himself up and rushed headlong towards the yellow target as Oley lowered it into the water. Two feet from the target, he suddenly jammed on the brakes by lowering his pectoral fins, and did a back flip out of the water, sending a spray of water over Oley, Dr Brown, and me. All three sharks in the pen began acting strangely, swimming erratically, fast then slow, every which way, bumping into each other as they turned.

The male lemon shark never recovered from this experience. He refused food offered in any way, wouldn't go near even a white target again, and died three months later. His skin wrinkled as he lost weight. His swimming movements changed completely, his body twisted, and he kept his head turned to one side with his body muscles contracted on that side. He swam slowly, always at the surface, his back slightly arched and his tail almost half out of the water. The long upper lobe of his tail flapped on the surface of the water.

'Maybe he sprained his back on that back flip,' Oley suggested. But then we noticed that on rare occasions the shark could straighten out.

We felt terrible about his death. For more than a year, he had been a part of our daily activities. We had examined hundreds of sharks by now, but it was very different to put the body of this lemon shark on the dock for a routine dissection. We did this after school hours because Tommy wanted to be there. The shark's liver was shrivelled and leathery. We towed the remains of this once beautiful creature some miles out into the gulf and watched it sink.

IV Divers and Sharks

Divers who work in the areas of the ocean where sharks are prevalent learn far more about these creatures in a few months than the most industrious scientist who never sets foot in the water could ever learn on land.

Sharks in their natural element are truly the most incredible creatures. Their awesome beauty of shape and movement defies apt description, for to see a great shark in the ocean, gliding weightlessly through his blue world, is not only a visual sensation but an emotional one as well. The full impact of the experience can be completely appreciated only by the people present at the time and to be present one must be able to dive.

Stories about sharks and divers are always more exciting than, say, stories about game fishermen and sharks. For a start, the reader knows that there is no way the shark is going to attack and eat the fisherman. In diver and shark stories, however, there is always the strong element of impending disaster. Divers do get attacked by sharks and sometimes lose their lives as a result. In spite of this, many divers, ourselves included, feel no animosity towards sharks. In fact, we seek them out whenever the opportunity presents itself. They are always exciting companions and good photographic subjects.

Newcomers to the sport of diving are generally somewhat apprehensive about sharks. This is perfectly normal. It takes time to adjust to something new and sharks are no exception. Actually, the diver who sees sharks frequently is fortunate indeed. We have great difficulty finding them. The only place we know of where potentially dangerous sharks are still very plentiful is the Coral Sea.

Of course, they must also abound in other remote areas but a constant supply of good sharks is no longer common near any heavily populated area. Fifteen years ago, fast-moving pelagic sharks were common all along the New South Wales coast. Today they are a rarity.

Jacques Cousteau and Hans Hass, those pioneers of the sport, must have seen some wonderful sights during their early years in diving. Even I can remember great packs of sharks off the coast as recently as twelve years ago. Now, they, along with most other big fish, have gone and it's only the diver who can know this, for it's only the diver who can see it for himself.

Reading or hearing about an event is never quite the same as seeing it personally. The big sharks of the world are a dying breed. While environmentalists fight for the sea mammals, it is hardly likely that they would side with the sharks whose reputation makes them so unpopular.

13

From *The Coast of Coral*

Arthur C. Clarke

In 1969, Ron and I met Arthur Clarke on board the *Terrier VII* off the coast of what was then Ceylon. Mr Clarke came aboard while we were trying to film sharks and marine life on the *Hermes*, a British aircraft carrier sunk by the Japanese in 180 feet of water during World War II.

I had read with pleasure many of his books and meeting the famous man in person left me shy and tongue-tied, two things from which I seldom suffer. Not only did I admire Mr Clarke as a writer of some of the world's best science fiction but I also respected him as a diver of great skill and experience. As so often happens when in the presence of someone you greatly admire, words failed me.

This segment from his book *The Coast of Coral* describes something which has happened to a great many divers, including Ron and me. I am immensely impressed with the truth and simplicity of his writing. No exaggeration or false drama, and this from a man famous for his imagination and dramatic stories of fiction.

The area where this incident occurred is off the reef at Heron Island, not far from a place we call the Bommie. We know the area well. For the past ten years, Heron Reef has been a national park, but before this, spearfishing was not only allowed but encouraged. Clarke's description of the sharks and their behaviour, both swimming free and after being speared, is excellent.

I was also interested to note that a shout from Arthur Clarke had no more effect on the shark than a shout from me, and is another example of one of the classic shark repellents failing.

Clarke's book is fine reading. It is honestly presented from cover to cover, yet retains a flow of excitement and adventure that would hold the interest of any reader.

■

We met no very large fish – above all, no sharks – but we did not expect to do so, for we were inside the boundary of the reef and in comparatively shallow water. When we were quite sure that we had a reasonably good chance of photographing anything that came along, we prepared to make our first dive over the edge of the reef. Mike had made one preliminary reconnaissance under bad conditions some days before. The water was still dirty after a recent storm; he had dived off the dinghy just to have a look around and had climbed hastily back into the boat with a very thoughtful expression.

'It's weird down there,' he admitted, 'and there's some big stuff moving around. It won't be safe until the water's clearer – you can't see what's coming at you now.'

I was content to take his word for it; there was no point in running unnecessary risks by diving in water which was too dirty for photography – and photographs were, after all, the main object of our expedition.

It was about an hour after noon, and on a falling tide, that we rowed out to the reef and tried our luck for the second time. I slipped quietly overboard, with the Leica strapped round my neck, and found myself drifting twenty feet above a dense thicket of stag's-horn coral. The anchor of our boat lay supported in the topmost branches of the petrified forest, with a few small fish playing around its stock.

Visibility was excellent; when, a few seconds later, Mike followed me into the water, we could see each other clearly when we were sixty feet apart. The sun, though it had passed its noonday peak, was still powerful enough to throw patches of dappled light on the coral beneath us.

There were some very large fish moving sedately over the sea bottom, but never venturing far from the shelter of some cave or cranny into which they could retreat if danger threatened. Keeping one eye on Mike, who was prowling around with his spear gun at the ready, I made several dives to the bottom to take close-ups of interesting coral formations. After a while I decided that there was a better way of reaching my goal than swimming, which used up a lot of energy and air. The anchor line provided a convenient stairway into the depths, so I flushed out my lungs, then filled them to bursting, and pulled myself hand over hand down to the sea bed.

When I arrived at the bottom, most of my reserve of air was still intact; I twined my legs around the anchor and relaxed in the water to survey the situation in comfort. I hoped that if I remained motionless for long enough, some of the larger fish would let their curiosity overcome their natural caution.

Nothing whatsoever happened for almost a minute, and I was just about to head back to the surface when the utterly unmistakable shape I had been hoping to see slipped into my field of vision. Thirty feet away a small shark, with a startlingly white tip on its forward dorsal fin, was sailing smoothly above the coral undergrowth. It was no more than five feet long – just about the right size for an introduction to the species. As soon as I had refilled my lungs, I began to stalk it with the camera, and had no difficulty in securing a couple of shots as it passed over sandy bottom and was silhouetted against the dazzling white of pulverized coral.

Then I surfaced and yelled to Mike, who was in the water some distance away. I tried to indicate with my arms the direction the shark was taking, and Mike set off towards it as if jet-propelled. When I again ducked my head under the surface, I had lost sight of the beast, and regretted my missed photographic opportunities. Almost at once, however, there was a flurry fifty feet away, and Mike emerged momentarily to yell, 'I've got him.'

Ignoring the excellent rule that one should swim quietly on the surface, without making too much of a splash, I stern-wheeled across to Mike at maximum acceleration. When I arrived on the spot, I found him using his gun to fend off a very angry shark, which was turning and snapping on the spear that had passed right through its body below the rear fins. Though its crescent-shaped mouth was only about six inches wide, I did not at all like the way in which its teeth kept grinding together in rage and frustration.

I took two hasty photos, then moved in close (or as close as I cared) with my own hand spear, to help push the beast away from Mike if it showed signs of coming to grips with him. He had swum slowly backwards towards the boat, towing the spear with one hand and using the discharged gun to keep the still violently wriggling shark at bay.

We had an acquaintance in the dinghy who had come along for the ride and seemed slightly taken aback when we drew alongside and yelled at him to help haul our captive aboard. He reached down and tried to grab the tail, which was about the only thing he could do – though even this is not recommended in the best circles, since sharks can curl round to snap at their own tails with no trouble at all. They also have skins like sandpaper, which further discourages contact with the bare hands.

We had managed to get the shark halfway out of the water when, in a sudden paroxysm of fury, it succeeded in tearing itself loose from the spear. I caught a final brief glimpse of it shooting away across the coral, apparently none the worse for its encounter. When I surfaced again I found that Mike had climbed into the boat and was doing a dance of rage, accompanied by suitable sound effects, which were being greatly admired by another boat-load of spearfishers, who had now arrived on the scene. He stated, in no uncertain terms, what would happen to this particular shark if he ever met it again, with or without speargun. He added several footnotes, containing information which would have surprised ichthyologists, about the ancestry and domestic behaviour of sharks in general. In fact, he managed to convey the distinct impression that he did not, at the moment, feel very kindly disposed towards sharks.

When we had succeeded in calming him down a little, we went back into the water and did a search for the weight belt he had lost during the battle. After five minutes' hunting, he was lucky enough to find it on a patch of sand, and this did something to restore his good humour. The loss of these weights would have been quite a serious matter, as without them it would have been difficult or even impossible for him to remain in effortless equilibrium at any depth. Though we had brought spares of all our other equipment, we had drawn the line at an extra ten or twenty pounds of lead, which somehow always seems to be even heavier than it actually is.

While engaged in the search for Mike's belt, I had swum a considerable distance against the prevailing current and had noticed that the water 'upstream' was much clearer than in the region where we had been operating. So we pulled up the anchor and rowed a hundred yards against the current to try our luck farther round the edge of the reef.

The character of the bottom had changed greatly, even in this short distance. Huge coral boulders, ten feet high, were spaced at irregular intervals through the blue-lit twilight. The water was also considerably deeper and much richer in fish life. Horned rhinoceros fish, coral trout, and grouper swarmed beneath us, playing hide-and-seek around the submerged hillocks when we tried to get close to them. I noticed a fine grouper, well over a hundred pounds in weight, moving along a valley below me, and surfaced to draw Mike's attention to it. As I did so, a large turtle, moving with surprising speed for so ungainly a beast, shot past me and disappeared into the depths. I had no opportunity of giving this information to Mike, however, for no sooner had I broken surface than he shouted, 'Shark,' and pointed back into the water.

For a moment I wondered if our earlier victim had been rash enough to return. It took only a second's glance to dispose of that theory.

This was a real shark – a good ten feet of ultimately streamlined power, moving lazily through the waters beneath us. His body was a uniform metallic grey, with no trace of markings. He seemed aware of our presence, for he was cruising in a wide arc as if wondering what to do about us. I swam slowly above and behind him, trying to get a picture every time he was in a good position. If I kept moving steadily towards him, I felt quite sure that he would not come at me; indeed, my only concern was that I might make too violent a move and frighten him away. I was far too lost in admiration of this beautiful creature – the first large shark I had ever met in clear water – to feel the slightest sense of alarm.

But then I saw something that made my blood run cold. Mike, apparently thirsting for revenge, had reloaded his speargun. He was getting into position to attack this monster which was bigger than both of us put together.

I shot up to the surface like a rocket, and, as soon as Mike came up for air, yelled at him, 'For God's sake – don't shoot.' The spearfishers in the boat fifty feet away heard every word; Mike, a yard from me, appeared to be stone-deaf. I followed him all the way down, making all the sign gestures I could think of to try to dissuade him, but it was no use.

Things sometimes happen so quickly under water that often one can never clearly recall the sequence of events. I cannot remember the actual moment when the gun was fired; I can only remember my vast relief when the spear missed, and the shark veered away from its course. It did not, however, show any signs of fright as the steel arrow whizzed past its nose; indeed, it swept round in a great circle and swam towards Mike, who had now reeled in his spear but – luckily – had not had time to reload the gun. As the shark came slowly up to him, Mike suddenly realized that it was about time he did something, and began to shout into the water in the approved textbook fashion. The shark took no notice at all, but continued its leisurely approach. Mike jabbed his empty gun in its general direction; still it came on. Not until it was about five feet away, and Mike could see its myopic eyes staring straight into his face mask, did it apparently decide that this was just another of those annoying and indigestible human beings and swing contemptuously aside. I caught a last glimpse of it, a blurred torpedo lit by the slanting sunlight, as it vanished along the reef.

We climbed back into the boat, and recriminations continued as we rowed homewards. Mike swore, not very convincingly, that he thought I wanted him to shoot the shark. I produced all the witnesses within earshot to prove the contrary, and loudly lamented the masterpieces my camera had lost.

14

From *Men Beneath the Sea: Conquest of the Underwater World*

Hans Hass

The romantic figures of the lean, bearded Hans Hass and his photogenic wife, Lotte, were proof to us that a dedicated man-and-wife team, and the sea, could be a way of life perhaps unequalled in this day and age. Hans Hass courageously records what he saw and believed. Like Captain Jacques Cousteau, Hass is a pioneer pacesetter in the underwater world.

Hans Hass has been diving for far longer than Ron and I, and to me has always been something of a hero – the man who did the things the rest of us only dreamed about. He has been diving and taking pictures almost since the beginning of skin diving, and has helped bring the world under the sea closer to the general public in an enjoyable and easily understood way through his books and films.

In this segment from his book *Men Beneath the Sea: Conquest of the Underwater World,* Hans touches on many subjects familiar to Ron and me, mostly talking of things which stimulate and excite sharks. One which must be of interest is that Hans claims some aggressive sharks can be frightened by loud underwater screams.

We have experienced limited success with this method, although the sharks we generally work with are probably of different species from those Hans has encountered. Sharks are completely unpredictable creatures and what works well on one as a repellent is just as likely to have no effect on another.

Hans refers to us filming *Blue Water, White Death,* 'leaving the cages and swimming around quite unconcerned among dozens of excited sharks, tapping them on the snout and treating them quite lightheartedly.' This must be how it appears in the film for Hass to mention it that way, but in reality it was quite the reverse. We were all very concerned, not only for our own safety but for each other. Behind my lighthearted taps to the shark's snout was every bit of power and strength that my 126-pound body could muster.

At that time I felt that I was fighting for my life, although afterwards, on the deck of the *Terrier VII,* we would all appear elated and happy. This was due to completing the dive without mishap and capturing the action on film.

Hans has based his comments on what seems to be quite solid evidence but was not in fact an accurate interpretation, and does serve to point out the dangers of a writer misinterpreting an event. Nowadays, Hans Hass is more interested in conservation of the marine animals than in filming them and works hard towards the banning of spearfishing on a worldwide basis.

In October 1984, Ron and I met Hans and Lotte Hass during a film festival in Lucerne, Switzerland. We were strolling through the old section of the town when I heard someone calling 'Taylors, Taylors, Valerie'. We turned around, and there he was, my beautiful hero coming towards us, arms outstretched in a gesture of friendship.

It was a wonderful moment in my life. Hans Hass is still the greatest diver the world has ever known, and ever will know. He was the first and the best. To see old films of him, movie camera in hand, filming feeding sharks, is outstanding. He had no breathing apparatus, no wet suit, no snorkel, no fins – just goggles, a camera and immense courage.

■

As for underwater films, the audience – and hence also the film distributors – are positively disappointed unless at some moment, accompanied by sinister music, the terrible spectre of a shark appears. On one of my own films, from which I financed the first *Xarifa* expedition, this was actually a stipulated condition. Every diver who can report being attacked by a shark finds a willing circle of listeners who automatically regard him as a hero. John D Craig, an American diver and professional film producer, declared. 'Every shark that is hungry or angry or both will attack a man.' This is simply not true. Cousteau was molested by sharks in the open sea off the Cape Verde Islands during his first visit to the tropics, and this obviously left him in a state of shock. In a book he later declared that the better acquainted one becomes with sharks, the less one knows about them. This story also gained wide acceptance, and is often quoted today as the quintescence of an expert's experience.

In an American film the hero (Gary Cooper) was accused in court by two old maids of being 'pixilated' and therefore unfit to testify. The two ladies meant by this that he had a screw loose – but defending counsel had an idea, and asked them if they regarded anyone else as 'pixilated'.

'Of course,' they replied at once, 'everybody – except for the two of us.'

'Even his Honour the judge?'

'Yes, he's pixilated, too.' And the man was acquitted. It is no different with the 'unpredictability' of sharks. Of course there are surprises, but they are extremely rare and certainly not characteristic of these creatures. My reply to Cousteau's sibylline pronouncement would be: 'The more thoroughly one investigates sharks, the better one knows them.'

The behaviour of sharks – as of any other creature – is governed by instincts which are activated by optical, acoustic, olfactory, or other stimuli. Konrad Lorenz speaks of a 'parliament of instincts' in which, according to the 'majority vote' of the moment, now one and then another governs behaviour. This means in practice that animals respond more strongly to, or actively seek, first one stimulus then another. A hungry creature responds primarily to those stimuli which make him aware of his prey, one which is amorously disposed will respond primarily to those of his sexual partner. With sharks, there are four groups of stimuli which lead them to their prey.

They can detect disturbances of the water, that is to say, fluctuations in pressure, from a great distance – you can observe this if you drop anchor or dive into the water near the edge of a reef. Often it takes no more than a few seconds before sharks are in sight. However, they usually keep at a considerable distance, make one or two circuits, and then as a rule, if nothing further occurs to excite them, disappear immediately. As I wrote in my first accounts, they behave like 'policemen, looking to see what's going on'. A dynamic explosion in which fish are stunned or killed also creates a visual stimulus; if it is repeated frequently, sharks snap at fish and associate them with the detonation. In Greece in 1942 we were amazed at how quickly sharks gathered where there was fishing with dynamite. Normally a diver never catches sight of a shark there, but we saw specimens over thirteen feet long.

Sharks are especially sensitive to vibrations of the water caused by the struggles of a fish which is wounded or otherwise in distress. In response to this stimulus, sharks frequently swim in direct attack until they are close to the struggling creature. Every fisherman knows that any fish he catches in the tropics must be landed quickly, or he is likely to lift only a fish head out of the water. The rest, the sharks have snatched away. For underwater hunters, this constitutes – as we found in 1939 – a serious danger, and this is how accidents have already happened. The target of such attacks may well be the fish, but if the underwater hunter is holding it, then of course he himself may also get bitten.

Before Jack McKenney became editor of *Skin Diver*, he worked for three years as a diving instructor at Freeport on Grand Bahama, near Florida. In all that time, so he told me, he saw only about fifteen sharks. In the very last week he went fishing with a friend. It was past three o'clock in the afternoon, and they were harpooning fish. A grey shark suddenly appeared. Jack said: 'I had my camera with me, and I thought to myself, "Fine, now at last I'll get a good picture." ' But the shark swam off again. Then Jack harpooned another fish – back came the shark and snapped at it. 'I could hear his teeth grating on the hook, and I thought, "Help!" Then he came straight at me – I only had the harpoon – I thrust it at his head. He swam away and came back again. The third time I missed him, and he grabbed the harpoon only so far from my hand.' Jack showed me; it was about eight inches. 'I almost had heart failure!' The friend meanwhile had dropped the net with the fish. Two more grey sharks appeared. 'The one with my harpoon in his mouth probably thought I didn't taste too good. He swam down and paid no more attention to anything but the net with the fish. Meanwhile we swam ashore.'

So harpooning big fish in areas frequented by sharks is not without danger. Even in the Mediterranean there have been attacks, one of which had a particularly tragic end. On 2 September 1962, the pioneer Italian diver and distinguished underwater photographer Maurizio Sarra, harpooning grouper near Terracina on the Italian coast, was fatally wounded by a shark. Here is another case:

In the summer of 1964 Al Giddings and French Le Roy, two outstanding American divers, were diving off some islands north of San Francisco. They were leading a team of skin divers who went down in several parties. Numerous fish were harpooned. Suddenly Al Giddings who was just fetching his camera from the boat, heard shrill screams and saw someone floundering about on the surface. As quickly as he could, he swam towards him – and saw to his astonishment that it was not one of the pupils, but his partner Le Roy. A shark had wounded him. The sea was smooth, and just as he got to Le Roy an enormous tailfin appeared directly underneath the victim. Al Giddings said: 'Le Roy told me later that that was the most terrifying moment for him, because he could see in my eyes what I saw.' The great shark made another grab at Le Roy's leg, and dragged him under water. When Le Roy came up again, Giddings grasped his companion from behind by his air cylinders, for Le Roy was now flailing wildly about, as though demented. Giddings had the presence of mind to release his weighted belt and dragged Le Roy back to the boat. Every moment he expected a fresh attack, but none came. Le Roy was pulled on board, minus a sizable piece of his thigh. A tourniquet was applied and a helicopter summoned by radio. No one had even seen the shark, for Le Roy was already on the surface when unexpectedly attacked from behind, and Al Giddings lost his diving mask when he rushed to his aid. Here too there is no doubt that the harpooned fish had attracted the big shark, and the smell of blood had made it aggressive. The second stimulus which activates predatory behaviour in sharks is the smell of blood. In collaboration with Eibl-Eibesfeldt, I made an exhaustive study of this phenomenon in the Maldives in 1957. Near a steep ridge where we knew there were sharks, we killed some fish and hid them among the corals. In only about five minutes the smell of blood had spread far enough to attract sharks from the open sea outside our range of vision. They behaved in an obviously excited manner, darting about and poking their snouts right under the coral in search of the source of the blood. They were very perseverant and most of them found the hiding place. How utterly this olfactory stimulus dominates the shark is shown by instances where bathers have been bitten and gallant rescuers have brought them out of the water. These rescuers have hardly ever been wounded themselves, for the shark, if it continued the attack, bit only the person already wounded. Our experiments also produced the same results. At first we were wary, but we soon saw that the bleeding fish hidden in the coral, usually only two or three yards from us, were in effect our protectors. Eventually, up to ten sharks were squabbling over the prey and taking not the slightest notice of us. The calmness with which I filmed this scene indicates how safe we felt. True, Eibl-Eibesfeldt declared that the sharks showed more aggressiveness towards him, but this may have been because he was the one who had harpooned the fish and taken them off the spear, so the smell of blood was on his hands.

These observations are important for shipwrecked men. In areas where there are sharks, persons who are bleeding undoubtedly run the danger of being attacked, especially in tropical waters. But uninjured people in the vicinity need not despair; if attacks take place near them, this doesn't in the least mean that they will automatically be the next victims.

In this connection the account of Flight-Lieutenant A. A. Reading, who drifted in the open sea for sixteen hours after coming down east of the Wallis Islands, in the central Pacific, is instructive. When the plane crashed he was unconscious, but his radio officer, E. H. Almond, dragged him out of the aircraft. Almond, however, was unable to salvage the dinghy. The two men tied themselves together with a cord. Almond was wearing only shorts. 'In about half an hour,' reported Reading, 'there were already sharks swimming round us, but for an hour nothing happened. Suddenly Almond said he had felt something bump against his right leg, and it was beginning to hurt. I told him to climb up on my back and keep the leg out of the water, but before he could do so the sharks attacked him again. We were both forced under water for a second.' Five sharks now surrounded them, and the water was red with blood. Reading went on: 'He showed me his leg; not only was his right foot covered with bites, his left hip also was badly gashed. He didn't feel any great pain, but I noticed how every time the sharks went for him, his whole body twitched. Finally I grabbed my binoculars and struck at the creatures as they swam by. Within a few seconds they attacked again. Once more we were dragged under, and this time I became separated from Almond.' Reading received a blow across his right cheek from one of the sharks, but this was all that happened to him. He saw how his companion was hemmed in by the sharks, his head already under water. Then the body drifted away, encircled by sharks. 'Every now and then I felt one at my feet...' So Reading drifted for several hours, until at midnight he was picked up by a patrol boat – uninjured. Other accounts of shipwrecked men and of airmen shot down read very similarly. If you consider that sharks are predators and possess a murderous set of teeth, it's really rather surprising how hesitant they are to make use of these weapons. In the case of Reading and Almond, the fact that Almond was wearing shorts may have been significant. He was attacked, but Reading was not; the sharks which swam past so close obviously missed the smell of skin which provoked the attack.

Other stimuli of aggressive behaviour may be found in the sphere of optical perception. The assertion that sharks' eyesight is poor has been proved on closer investigation to be false, and they are no longer believed to be colour-blind. It used to be claimed that Negroes were attacked less often than men with light skin, but experiments by the American biologist Hobson on Eniwetok Atoll with three different species of shark produced exactly the opposite result. From a raft he lowered into the sea two identical baits, one darkened with a pigment to which, as tests had shown, sharks were not responsive. Out of 172 tests the dark bait was taken first in 72 per cent of cases overall, and in 82 per cent of cases when the sky was clear and sunny. Admittedly, the observer, who was on the bottom in a cage, pointed out that in the given conditions the black bait was more clearly distinguishable from the background. The sharks always came out of deep water from the same direction, swimming against the current. Certainly these results do show that visual impressions also play a part. If a shark is attracted by pressure waves or smell to within sight of an object, then such stimuli are decisive factors in its predatory behaviour. On the other hand, if a shark encounters a diver by chance without its aggressiveness being stimulated by blood or by a flurry of fish, as a rule it keeps well away from him, eyes him, and perhaps cruises round him, then swims on its way.

The final stimulus which governs aggressive behaviour in a shark is the taste of the object under attack. Hobson soaked fish in ethyl alcohol for four days and then rinsed them for three hours in seawater. Then he offered them to the sharks together with normal fish, once again lowering them from a raft. In every case both baits were taken – and each time the one that had been rendered tasteless was spat out. So after pressure waves, smell, and optical stimuli have evoked the shark's predatory behaviour, it is ultimately flavour which determines whether or not the predator really bites into its prey and swallows it. In earlier accounts it was claimed that sharks would swallow anything, and that even brushes and the like had been found in shark's bellies. This may well be true when they're gobbling up refuse thrown overboard from ships, but it's probably not the general rule. When Hobson offered the sharks fish made of wood or other material, they simply sniffed at them and turned up their noses.

How then, when all is said and done, must a diver behave if a shark – as happens only in rare and exceptional cases, unless it is actually being hunted – should approach him? It has often been recommended that he keep still, this is what pearl divers do. As with most predators on land, anything motionless scarcely attracts attention, even if it is conspicuous by its shape or colour. Back in 1939, in the West Indies, we found that approaching sharks can be put to flight if you swim straight at them. This method may not be to everyone's taste, but it works excellently. In this way I have frightened away even very big sharks, over thirteen feet long. Here again we find the same reaction displayed by land predators. A swiftly and purposefully approaching body inspires flight; man also reacts in the same way.

Another 'weapon' which we discovered at that time has even found its way into cartoons. Quite by chance, we discovered that sharks which come storming in at top speed after a fish has been speared can be scared off by shouting into the water. Later on, when investigating the death of the Australian prime minister, Harold Holt, who disappeared in the sea near Melbourne in 1967, I found in his house a framed cartoon which showed him swimming under water and shouting at a shark which bore the inscription 'taxpayer'. The caption said, 'But you can't chase this one away by shouting!' We have observed this effect with reef sharks in the Red Sea, the Indian Ocean, and the Pacific, and many other well-known divers have confirmed our experience – for example, Jim Oetzel, Ron Clark, Rodney Jonklaas, R. H. Burton, and others. Wally Gibbins one of Australia's oldest and most daring pioneers of diving, had a special method of harpooning sharks, in which he would fasten the head of the spear by a long rope to a tyre floating on the surface. The harpooned shark dragged the tyre behind it and so exhausted itself, while the divers followed. Naturally enough, Gibbins and his companions were frequently attacked. Gibbins wrote: 'You can easily see when things are getting serious from the way a shark behaves. In my experience the best thing to do then is to take your stance and wait until the shark is about six feet away, then suddenly stretch out your arms and legs, and shout. The nearer the shark, the more effective the shout.' This tallies exactly with our experience. On the other hand, anyone trying to frighten a shark swimming by at a distance of thirty feet or more is hardly likely to succeed.

True, as we discovered back in 1942, there are exceptions. In Greece, the sharks that came racing along after dynamite explosions did not react at all to shouting. This was because they were accustomed to much louder noises. Nor can it be expected that sharks which frequent the vicinity of public bathing beaches, where people often shout in the water, or those which follow ships and get used to the noise of their screws, will react to shouts. When diving gear is used, the mouthpiece makes it difficult to shout and muffles the sound. With oxygen-recycling equipment, which makes no noise, this is less critical than with compressed-air gear, when air bubbles are regularly emitted into the water. Even the bubbles which suddenly appear with the shout (when a mouthpiece is worn they come out of the corners of one's mouth) may play their part in the deterrent effect. Earlier divers' accounts often mention that sharks are frightened of air bubbles.

We discovered in the Azores in 1953 that the deep-sea white-fin sharks in general do not react to shouts. I observed the same thing in the rare white shark and also the tiger shark. Philippe Cousteau, in a book about sharks written jointly with his father, said that to advise anyone to scare off a shark by shouting was 'criminal'. To this I can only say that very many other people have witnessed its effectiveness – with the limitations mentioned above, of course.

Unexpected behaviour does occur with sharks just as with any other creature. On many occasions sharks – even quite small ones – suddenly swam at us for no apparent reason. If one then stays still – my wife also has followed this rule – the shark will turn away of its own accord. Obviously this isn't a genuine attack – what would be the motive? I think it's a question of territory. Intruders are deterred and chased out of the domain. Here, too, Hobson's experience is instructive. In many instances he observed that sharks carried out deterrent measures against grouper and snapper which competed for their prey – but also against divers. He called them 'warning passes'.

A totally unexpected reaction was observed by two American divers, Ron Church and James Stewart, near La Jolla, on the coast of southern California. They were swimming in a channel between two reefs when a shark came straight between them from the direction of the shore. First it turned towards Ron, who photographed it, then towards Jimmy. Once again it was startled and swam off a little way. Then it turned round, looked back, and dashed straight at Stewart and bit him in the arm. This shark was little more than six feet long.

As investigations with land animals have shown, such unexpected reactions occur either when an impulse cannot be worked off or when two impulses run counter to each other and the animal thus becomes confused. Then we get 'flash behaviour'. The energy of thwarted instinctive behaviour flashes across, as it were, into other channels. The animal then behaves in a way which is not at all motivated by the actual situation.

I have already pointed out in my earliest books that sharks are very sensitive, indeed almost high-strung. The American biologist Eugenie Clark, who for ten years was head of an institute in Florida dedicated to the study of shark behaviour made an observation which very clearly supports my view. During tests in a water tank to measure the intelligence of sharks, she trained a female and a male to strike with their heads a board lowered into the water, thus setting off a mechanism which rang a bell. The sharks received their food near the board – and later at points farther and farther away. The two sharks, one eight feet and the other ten feet long, became accustomed to this procedure and regularly rang a bell. 'Then,' writes Eugenie Clark, 'unwittingly I made a decision with tragic consequences.' As it was still debatable whether sharks were colour-blind or not, she painted the white board yellow. When it was lowered, the male shark raced towards it as usual, but pulled up suddenly two feet away from it by lowering its pectoral fins, and leaped backwards out of the water. The other sharks in the aquarium thereupon swam madly to and fro, colliding with each other. The shark 'never recovered from this experience. He refused food offered in any way, wouldn't go near a white target again, and died three months later.'

A further observation by Clark is no less enlightening. On 27 July 1958, not far from her institute, a shark only six feet long bit an eight-year-old boy whose leg had to be amputated immediately. As she discovered, the accident happened at very low tide, in a lagoon in which the shark had obviously become trapped. When low tide came, it could not get back across the sand bank into the sea. This state of confusion may, she thinks, have been the reason why when it saw the boy's light-coloured legs in the cloudy water, it swam in biting. This incident could at a pinch be compared with the attack on Jim Stewart – who blamed his glittering mask as the critical factor.

One species of shark which can perhaps with justification be described as a 'killer shark' will almost certainly be exterminated by man sooner or later – the white shark *(Carcharodon)*. With a behaviour pattern different from other kinds of shark, this creature really is dangerous to man and hence, presumably, is doomed to extinction. The white shark lives in the open sea and only occasionally approaches the coast. How rarely this creature puts in an appearance is shown by the fact that Peter Gimbel, Ron Taylor, and Stan Waterman, who were making a film about the white shark, cruised for six months between Africa and Australia and killed countless creatures for bait before they finally managed to entice a specimen out of the deep.

A fatal accident caused by a white shark occurred on 14 June 1959, near the Scripps Institute, in La Jolla. The victim, Robert Pamperin, was a thirty-three-year-old engineer, an enthusiastic underwater hunter and diver. Accompanied by a less experienced friend, he was diving for abalone, which have to be pried off the seabed with a flat iron bar. The bar is pushed quickly under the opened shell before it can close and batten onto the rock. Pamperin was towing along with him an inflated tyre, from which hung a bag for the abalone. He was wearing pink swimming trunks, a black face mask, and blue flippers. The two men set out from a rocky headland and went about fifty yards out from shore. Here the partner who was less good at diving decided to work in shallower water. Suddenly he heard Pamperin, about twenty yards away, cry for help. He turned quickly to see Pamperin being thrown straight out of the water, having already lost his face mask. Then the body disappeared under water. Quickly he swam in that direction and looked downward – the visibility was only about twenty-five feet. To his horror he saw a gigantic shark, which he estimated was more than twenty feet long. It was holding Pamperin round his middle in its mouth, shaking him to and fro, and lashing out fiercely with its tail fin. He tried to frighten the beast by shouts and movements, but in vain. Then he lost sight of them both, and swam as fast as he could to the shore, where he raised the alarm. Conrad Limbaugh, diving director of the Scripps Institute, was quickly on the spot with nine volunteers. For four and a half hours they searched the area with diving gear – but without success. Later, a helicopter spotted a blue flipper floating on the surface, and Pamperin's tyre with two abalone in the bag, was found drifting in the sea. As Conrad Limbaugh, at that time perhaps America's most experienced diver, confirmed, fish had been harpooned in the area a little earlier.

On 14 June 1950, I myself was attacked by a white shark near the landing stage of the Sanganeb reef, in the Red Sea eleven miles north-east of Port Sudan. This specimen was thirteen feet long and came steadily towards me, like a machine. I had been filming smaller shark and only saw the creature when it was very close to me. I was at the top of a vertical face of the reef, where I was crouching on projecting coral at a depth of about 50 feet. To lure sharks we had chopped fish into pieces and tossed them into the sea near the edge of the reef. When I noticed the creature, it was already too late to reach for my spear, which was floating above me, fastened to my shoulder by a loop. I gave a scream, as loudly as I could – but this shark did not react, so I was left with only my hands with which to ward off the great head. It must be emphasized that the creature displayed not the slightest excitement. The light-grey colossus swam quite slowly in a straight line along the wall directly towards me – just as if I were any old chunk of meat it wanted to snap up. When the snout was right in front of me, I punched at the back of its mouth, in the region of the gills. It turned away and circled round. The unexpected movement directed against it had produced the reaction of flight. Then steadily and unswervingly it came at me again – no slower and no faster. In the meantime I had had time to reach for my spear, and I thrust the point at its head. It turned away. Now, however, I was attacked by the other shark, which I had been filming earlier, and which up till then had been only curious but by no means aggressive. It was about ten feet long and wanted a piece of me too – an example of mood transference, of the infectiousness of predatory behaviour. I could not possibly defend myself on two sides, so I scrambled up the wall as fast as my flippers would take me, to where my three colleagues, including Lotte, were waiting on the ridge and had witnessed the whole episode. The result of my flight was that the two sharks followed me with equal speed, but we were lucky, for it was just low tide. On the top of the reef the water was barely eighteen inches deep, and all four of us fled into this shallow zone, where the creatures could not follow us. They swam up and down close to the edge, clearly excited; then they calmed down again and disappeared from our sight.

The white shark may possess a differently developed set of innate reactions from other sharks. This could be related to the creature's size, also perhaps to its life in the open sea. For this kind of predator, the motivating stimuli scarcely need to be differentiated, and those inhibitions which would make them approach strange objects with caution are superfluous. It is known from finds of fossilized teeth that the now presumably extinct ancestors of this variety of shark reached the incredible length of over eighty feet. According to reconstructions, the mouth must have been big enough for a man to stand up in. For such a mighty predator, almost anything in the wide ocean that came its way would be potential prey. This would explain why this creature, in contrast to the coastal sharks, behaves so mechanically, and automatically swims up to attack even a being that is strange to it – a human being.

Other species of shark known to have caused fatal accidents in Australia and South Africa are the tiger shark, the mako shark, the blue shark, and the hammerhead. These species too reach considerable size, and are rarely seen near the coast. Compared to today's figures for traffic accidents on land, however, the danger which these sharks represent is very slight. In both countries, watchtowers have been erected to guard popular beaches; if a sizeable shark is sighted, a warning bell is rung. In the last ten years, underwater hunters – especially in the Australian coasts – have killed many sharks, some of them quite large, with shark clubs which have explosive heads. Wide-meshed nets of fine nylon have also proved very effective, for the sharks do not notice them; they get their heads stuck in them, finally becoming so entangled that they perish. Presumably up to 90 per cent of the sharks killed in this manner were harmless. Still, whereas Australia previously had two deaths a year to complain of – an extremely small proportion of the hundreds of thousands of swimmers, divers, and surfers – the sharks there have now been eliminated over wide stretches. However, as a bogey, a jealously guarded property of journalism, films, and adventure books, the shark is still an effective box-office draw. This may have been acceptable hitherto, but now, when sporting divers take to the water in such large numbers, things are different. What makes money for one man may endanger others, even cost them their lives.

For, as has been said before, the greatest danger for divers is panic, a reaction inspired by fear. In this sense, misleading information is not only dangerous but actually 'criminal'. For example, films which Philippe Cousteau has produced with his father include scenes of a regular bloodbath taking place around cages containing divers. Close-ups show how the sharks enticed in this way attack greedily. What else would one expect? This keeps the shark's image as a 'blood-thirsty killer' alive and, moreover, satisfies the audience. The danger of such presentations is that with sharks – as with land predators – fear and flight excite interest and aggressive behaviour. Although according to present-day experience divers are hardly in danger even when a sizeable shark comes in sight, panic behaviour can actually attract these creatures and indeed arouse their aggressive instinct.

For this reason it is also important to oppose trick photography. On 7 June 1968, *Life* published a sensational story which showed most convincingly a diver being bitten in the chest by a shark. In Germany this was copied by *Stern* and in Britain by *Weekend Mail*. According to this report the accident had happened during filming off Isa Mujeres, on the Mexican coast. I received letters from there to the effect that not a word of the report was true. It then turned out that these pictures were intended as publicity for a film. A dead shark was fastened to a diver in appropriate positions, and at the same time red dye was released from a bag. Dewey Bergman, an American diver and head of an organization for arranging diving expeditions, spent a whole year clearing up this case, and eventually *Life* had to admit the hoax in the magazine *Skin Diver*. The editor wrote: 'What we took to be an unusual picture story proved to be a fabrication ...' Typically, however, *Life* never let on about it in its own magazine, nor did *Stern* or *Weekend Mail*. But thanks to this publicity the film, in the making of which the accident was supposed to have happened, was a box-office sellout.

Divers in cages, surrounded by many sharks attracted by blood, were shown in Peter Gimbel's film about the white shark. But to the credit of this film, it must be said that the next scene showed these divers – Ron and Valerie Taylor, Stan Waterman, and Gimbel himself leaving the cages and swimming around quite unconcernedly among dozens of excited sharks, tapping them on the snout and treating them quite lightheartedly. When Eibl-Eibesfeldt and I ran feeding experiments without cages, we had the same experience, namely that the creatures concentrated entirely on the source of the blood. I do not seek to belittle the extraordinary courage of the divers I have named, for when they took their pictures there were far more sharks about, and besides, they were filming out at sea. Nevertheless, what must be emphasized about all films of this kind is that such orgies of greed represent totally untypical situations, created artificially, which give no information at all about the normal behaviour of sharks.

A weapon every diver should carry is a stick about four feet long with a moderately sharp point, which he can fasten to his shoulder by a loop. If the unusual should in fact occur, and a shark should become a nuisance, it can be fended off. To sum up, I can only repeat that as long as he does not spear any big fish, the sporting diver who makes a descent off tropical coasts need hardly worry about being molested by sharks. It is far more likely that he will have the disappointment of not seeing any sharks at all.

15

The Mesh Suit Experiment

Valerie Taylor

'I swung around startled as the shark grabbed my arm above the elbow. White triangular teeth crushed my flesh as they sawed across the steel links – tearing, pulling, moving, bite by awesome bite, down my arm.

I tried to pull away, but the animal was relentless in its attack. Horrified, I watched as the cuff of my protective glove became enmeshed in those terrible teeth. I pushed my hand forward, but too late. The glove pulled away.

My naked wrist was inside the shark's jaw. What a thin vulnerable looking wrist it was. Almost without thought, I thrust my mesh covered left hand between the jaws, covering its unprotected partner with steel.

Helpless now because both hands were trapped beyond the teeth, I screamed, silently to all but myself, not once, but many times. No longer able to keep my instincts under control, I pulled my hands free, taking the force of the bite on my left wrist. Pain, cold as ice, green blood squirting. I grabbed the wounded fingers and watched in amazement as the prehistoric creature moved away, black target eyes watching as it swallowed my glove. Silently the other sharks circled. Ron filmed, Howard filmed. As I swam towards our charter boat, the *Sand Dollar*, I thought, "Its my third bite. Everything comes in threes, now I am safe." I was almost happy.'

This extract from my diary is dated 24 June, 1981. My husband Ron and myself were working on a *National Geographic* hour special about sharks.

The following story tells how I came to be testing myself as human shark bait in the deep cold waters off the Californian coast. It is about an idea my husband had back in 1967 and how that idea finally became a reality. Most important of all is how well that idea worked, making it possible for man at last to dive in most of the world's oceans without fear of mutilation or possible death from a shark attack.

■

7 June, 1980

We are 25 miles off San Diego, California, and once again plan to test our mesh suits, this time against oceanic blue sharks *(Crionace glauca)*. In the open ocean, this shark is a known attacker of man and, unlike so many other members of its family, quite fearless around divers. Fortunately, they are deep water sharks not found close to shore or populated beach areas.

We had been chumming with minced mackerel for two hours. The *Sea World* drifted lazily on a smooth Pacific swell. Our friend Milt Shedd, who owns the *Sea World* is very generous giving us use of his beautiful boat. We have rarely worked from such comfort, and it made a wonderful change from our small dinghy.

We have in the past worked with blue sharks in this area. Living in the deep oceans as they do, these sharks have not developed a fear of man and approach the diver without hesitation. This lack of fear should make it easier for us to coax them into a biting mood.

Already several sleek shapes, blue against darker blue, are patrolling the stern. As the water is cold, I suit up in my thickest wet suit. The jacket fitted just fine, but the pants wouldn't squeeze over my hips, so I didn't bother with them. At the time all I wanted to do was get in the water. I was excited, rushing a little I guess, not really being careless, but not wanting to hold the proceedings up either.

Looking back, I realise the enormous risks I was taking by only wearing half a suit, but at the time I was quite confident in my ability to handle the situation. For a while I had forgotten the cardinal rule of shark attacks. You never see the one that gets you.

Several sharks came and went. Blue against blue they circled, black target eyes expressionless as a dead man's, watching. What were they thinking – these predators from a bygone era – could they think? Did they know how helpless we really were? From the great depths they had come, lured to us by the smell of blood and the promise of food. I drifted gently in the cold wet world; an alien, but at home waiting for the attack. We all waited. Jeremiah in Ron's mesh suit. Ron unprotected, camera ready.

It came quite casually, eyeing the mackerel I was offering. As the menacing membrane rose, I withdrew the fish and offered my arm. Blind now, instinct took control. The shark tore at my elbow, chewed down my wrist and munched on my hand. I thought 'my hand is unprotected except for the mesh'. I waited for the blood, I waited for the pain. There was none. Just wrenching and pressure. I beat the shark off. It was as though it had never happened. Ron filmed on, the sharks circled, history was being made. Another took a fish from my hand and another, possibly encouraged by this, grabbed my left arm. She began vibrating in the traditional way of most triangular saw-tooth sharks. There was pressure, but no pain, though I must admit to a prick or two where her very fine lower teeth penetrated the mesh. Being pulled about was unpleasant as I lacked the strength to hold my own. Time and time again, I allowed the sharks to maul my arms. Several, unnoticed, initially chewed elsewhere on my suit. One nuzzled up under my arm in a fruitless attempt at reaching a vulnerable part. Without Ron's movie footage, I would hesitate to write this, lest people think my imagination a little extreme.

Ron was quickly out of film. I stayed in the water so Jeremiah could take still pictures. Within a minute one of the larger sharks approached unnoticed from above, grabbed me by the head and shook me back and forth rather briskly. It was really quite horrible. Water leaked into my mask and I had difficulty repelling the brute.

Jeremiah stopped taking stills and started beating the shark's head with his camera. Fortunately, this had the desired effect, though perhaps my saviour should have been a little less gallant and more commercial. He missed out on some very fine still pictures. It took me a few seconds to recover from this unexpected shake-up. My neck continued to feel rather disjointed, but a shark suddenly chewing on my arm had me moving again. My arms were becoming painful in the joints from so much pulling around, and I knew my neck was going to be a problem. However, nothing bad enough to cause me to leave the water. Although my legs received the occasional bump, the sharks definitely concentrated on my torso, probably because I was holding whole fish in my hand.

Ten minutes later Ron was back with a freshly loaded camera. Several good blues came in, sunlight rippling over their bodies. I endeavoured to allow only the largest sharks to bite as they would look better on camera.

Two or three nice specimens swam close eyeing my fish longingly, but they refused to attack. I felt sure they were our first sharks and had learnt through experience that there was nothing to be gained by trying to eat this strange hard-scaled creature. Trying to force my arm into their mouths had them clamping their lips and gills tight. It has been our experience that sharks, like many wild animals, learn very quickly from experience. In fact we believe that sharks can learn a simple lesson faster than most other marine animals, particularly if the motivation for learning is based on food.

Fortunately, several newcomers came up from the depths and did all the right things. One even chewed around my chest without causing any problems, but I had to kick several away from my legs. By now I was beginning to feel cold and it was with relief that I saw Ron indicating that he was out of film. Cold tends to slow down my concentration and my reflexes become sluggish. Instead of sharks, I start thinking of hot showers and coffee, which could be dangerous.

Back on board, everyone was very excited. Against small to

medium size sharks the idea definitely worked. We had discovered a method of protecting a person against not only possible shark attack, but also attack from other dangerous marine and land creatures, such as piranha, wolves, lions, mad monkeys, men with knives, just to name a few.

Divers working in shark infested waters would be safer in a mesh suit and also feel more confident, thereby doing their job better and with greater efficiency. It could do for diving what the parachute did for flying. Make it safer.

It is amazing that Ron, who had this idea way back in 1967, should have waited so long before putting it into practice, but then a lot of inventions lie dormant in the inventor's mind until some small thing triggers it into a reality.

16
Riding a Shark

Valerie Taylor

All divers who love the sport and thrill of adventure must long to meet a whale shark. It is, without doubt, one of the big highs associated with skin diving – and one of the rarest.

When we found our whale shark, Ron had been trying to film sea lions for an episode in a television series called 'Skippy, the Bush Kangaroo'. The sea lions were swimming and playing close to the rocks in very turbulent water, which was unsuitable for filming. We tried to coax them out away from all the breaking waves, but they were having so much fun, they ignored all our efforts.

If they had cooperated and followed us into clearer water we would have stayed with them, instead of giving up and heading back to shore. Fate, which had seemed so unkind, sent us right into the path of the whale shark, and what seemed a failure became one of the greatest successes of our diving career.

Neither Ron nor I are very proud of our initial impulse to kill the creature, but it was at a time when we genuinely believed, along with most other divers, that all sharks were potential attackers and that the only good one was a dead one. Time and much more experience has shown us that we were wrong.

Whale sharks are not common; you could search for a lifetime and never see one. We had never seen one before and we haven't seen another since.

The sight of a 50-foot long shark has different effects on different people. One diver we know, when confronted with a 35-foot whale shark, grabbed his diving companion and held him like a shield before the shark. It is only ignorance that causes such fear. Whale sharks are harmless, gentle plankton eaters, not given to attacking large creatures, marine or otherwise.

Unfortunately, they do have a tendency to scratch their backs on floating objects, such as boats. This habit can be very disconcerting and dangerous for passengers on the boat chosen. In a case like this, the only defence is to move away from the area.

We remember our ride on the whale shark as one of the most exciting and outstanding encounters we have ever had at sea.

■

Ron Taylor, John Harding, our diving assistant, and myself were pounding shoreward through a heavy northerly slop. It was a nasty day and we were returning after an unsuccessful filming trip to Seal Rocks off the New South Wales coast, where heavy seas had made work impossible. John was standing up on the bow of our 14-foot aluminium dinghy trying to keep the nose down and soften the ride when he called out that there was something big and dark in the water ahead.

The boat crested a wave and, suddenly, we could all see it, a huge shape moving along just below the surface. A black dorsal fin intermittently broke through the waves. We were all on our feet now staring in amazement. There could be no mistake. It was a shark.

The boys thought, because of its size it must be a white pointer, the most dreaded shark in the world and responsible for attacks on four of our diving friends. Ron decided that, because we had to continue working in the area the next day, we should try to kill it with our powerheads.

There was a mad scramble in the boat as we all frantically searched for our diving gear, bullets, powerheads, and cameras. Ron felt that the best possible method to bring about a quick death would be for him and John to fire simultaneously, both trying for the spine. The water was only around 160 feet deep in this area and, once the shark was killed, it would sink. Ron could then, using scuba, recover it and we could tow our victim into shallow water and take photographs. I was to try to photograph the kill with my still camera.

If the pointer was not killed immediately, the shock of having two ·303 bullets enter its body at close range should frighten it into the depths where it would surely die from its wounds. At the very least, we should be able to frighten it away.

The boat was manoeuvred into position a few yards ahead of the monster. Ron cut the motor and we all jumped out, abandoning our boat to its own devices. I lay joggling on the surface, apprehensive in spite of the closeness of my armed companions, my eyes straining into the distance.

For a few seconds there was nothing, then, suddenly, like a tanker emerging from a fog, came a head so enormous it hardly seemed real. We hung suspended, powerheads dangling, as yard after yard of beautiful, spotted streamlined body flowed past. Before our amazed eyes was not the dreaded white pointer which we had foolishly thought to kill, but the largest shark in the world, the rare whale shark. Ron had dreamed of this moment for years and at last it had arrived, five miles out to sea, in a howling northerly gale. It could have been a cyclone for all we cared. Here was our shark, bigger and better than our wildest dreams. For the moment, fate was our friend.

Frantic with excitement, we scrambled back into the boat after photographic equipment. Fortunately, we had both movies and still cameras on board. The boys wanted me to look after the boat, but not on your life. I wasn't missing out on this experience; the boat could look after itself. It wouldn't come to much harm this far out to sea.

At first, we were hesitant as to the best approach. The shark, whom I called Wimpy in spite of her sex (she was a female), was 40 to 50 feet long, 7 or 8 feet through the widest part, and had a head the size of a double bed. All this was propelled through the water by a mackerel-type tail over 7 feet high. We knew it was a peaceful plankton-eating creature, but she was just so darn big.

I started by hanging onto her dorsal fin, then I moved up to her pectoral fin. She swam placidly on. The only time she showed any resentment to our attentions was when I accidentally put my hand in her eye. There was a sudden crash dive to a depth of around 50 feet, then a gradual return to the surface. John and I crawled all over our giant shark acting for Ron's camera. We knew she was the largest ever photographed anywhere in the world. Only three other divers that we knew of had ever photographed whale sharks, and we were familiar with their shots. Ours was by far the largest. To tell her correct size would be quite impossible, as the water visibility made it difficult to see all of her at once.

She seemed to be following a set course. We tried turning her back, but without effect. It was like trying to turn around a locomotive without rails. Some unknown destination beckoned her southward and nothing we puny humans could do was going to make any difference. To her we were no more than parasites sneaking a free ride and that's how she treated us, with complete disdain.

She had a very ugly head but rather beautiful body. Her skin was dark and spotted with white. Like all sharks it was very abrasive. John's legs received a nasty chafing when he rode on her tail. I looked into her mouth. A deep breath and I would have been sucked down that great rubbery-looking cavern without even touching the sides, a thought which made me move away to a safer position. Small parasites skated around her lips, scattering from my path. Like us, they were nothing but a nuisance to be completely ignored.

There were no remoras on her belly, which I thought rather unusual. Most large sea creatures carry these scavengers with them. Hard, bony ridges ran along her sides the length of her body. She was not so smoothly made as other sharks. More like a leopard shark or Port Jackson shark in appearance, only much, much bigger. One swipe from her mighty tail could smash us and our boat into little pieces. We tried riding her in every way we knew how.

John hung onto her tail and I onto John's ankles. With a mighty sweep, I was whipped through the water losing my face mask. After that, I took care to ride on the more static parts of her body. Fortunately for us, the shark was travelling with the wind and current so our dinghy was moving in the same direction. Every so often we could climb aboard our boat and move ahead of the whale shark, her dark shape easily seen even from a distance. Ron would take the opportunity to reload his movie camera, a tricky business in a small pitching dinghy, but the resulting footage would be well worth the effort. A chance like this might never come again. It was a once-in-a-lifetime experience.

We spent three and a half hours and travelled about five miles with our shark, but we could not stay with her forever. The cold was seeping through our wetsuits and into our bones. Lunch was six hours overdue. It was with reluctance, however, that we finally abandoned our shark to head back to shore. Her great black bulk could be seen moving away as we started the motor. I watched until her blackness vanished into the distance, swallowed under the turbulent ocean. Sad that our brief encounter had come to an end.

It was a long, cold, rough trip back, pounding into the teeth of the gale, but we didn't care. Our recent experiences were really worth it and I, for once, didn't mind the crashing boat and stinging spray. It had been a great day.

V Sharks that Attack

One thing that all authors of shark attack stories have in common is that they have to rely on second or thirdhand accounts as to what actually took place.

People's memories do differ: What one witness believes he saw can often be different from what another claims to have seen. It is to the credit of the experts who assess this information that when the final picture emerges, while not exactly correct in every detail, it certainly must be close to the truth.

Often, when I read the details surrounding an attack, particularly if by a shark whose habits are familiar to me, the possible motivation causing the incident is recognized. The reason for attacks on divers spearing fish are fairly apparent to most people. It is the smell of blood coupled with the vibrations of the wounded dying fish that attract the marauder who, by the time he reaches his quarry, has already begun to fall into a feeding pattern.

It is interesting that, while most spear fishermen I know have had speared fish torn from their floats, relatively few have been attacked themselves. This proves that the shark is not attracted to the human but rather to the fish which would be his natural prey. However, mistakes do occur and then we have a shark attack. The shark that bit Rodney Fox let him go and took the fish on his float line. It did not continue to attack.

In most cases, something must attract the shark to the potential victim. Sharks, not even the great white, don't swim around thinking that a human would be a nice animal to eat. If sharks really considered us to be good eating, in Australia at least, anyone entering the ocean would do so only at great risk. Surfboard riders often have their boards damaged by sharks, yet they themselves for the most part survive unmarked. I believe that sharks are curious about the large dead-looking objects floating on the surface and could go to investigate. Generally, they decide it's not what they want and swim away. Swimmers often fight off sharks. This would be impossible if the shark really meant business. With the majority of individual attacks recorded, it would seem that the attacker was merely investigating a strange object.

However, there are a number of cases where the shark attacked with a most positive attitude, tearing its victim to pieces, even when resistance had been strong. I feel the shark who attacks in this way is a very hungry shark whose desire to eat overrides all other instincts.

When a shark attacks a human, whatever the motivation is behind the attack, it is a terrible experience. The victim is hardly likely to care whether he was attacked by a hungry shark, a curious shark, or one who simply made a mistake. The horror and terror surrounding the act is always the same.

Australia's most recent shark attack occurred in shallow water between four and five metres deep, approximately 150 metres from shore. The victim, Shirley Anne Durden, was snorkelling for scallops with her husband Barry, and a friend Keith Coventry, out from Wiseman's Beach, Peake Bay, South Australia. Peake Bay had always been a popular picnic spot and the beach was dotted with families, including Mrs Durden's four children. It was a beautiful day with clear calm water. Keith Coventry told me that he was just swimming away after comparing his scallop catch with that of Mrs Durden, when he heard a stange sound, but definitely not as the papers reported, terrible screams. Keith told me, 'I heard a sound rather like a sharp groan. Turning around, I saw Shirley high above the surface. My first thought was how could she lift herself up like that, then a huge fin broke the water. There was some thrashing and the surrounding area turned dark. I instinctively swam towards Shirley, then thought, "Hey, what can I do? She's gone". Turning back, I saw Shirley's husband Barry standing 10 metres away on some submerged rocks about to enter the water. I swam to him and said, "Don't come in, a shark has taken Shirley, she's gone, completely gone". Barry was shattered. "I must go to Shirley. I must help her", he cried, but knowing it was useless, I held him back lest he meet the same terrible fate as his wife. We struggled for a minute, then turned towards the beach. The 120 metres looked like 120 kilometres. I don't think I have ever swum so hard in my life. One of my flippers came off, but I dared not hesitate to retrieve it. The thought of that huge black shark kept me going. A Mr Hirschausen, watching from a nearby cliff, raced to his dinghy at the water's edge. Within minutes, he and a friend had launched his boat and headed towards where he had last seen the woman. Her head and top torso were floating in a pool of blood, but before the rescuers could reach the remains, a great conical nose broke the surface and snatched them down, leaving nothing but empty blood-stained water. A huge search was organized, but only one blue flipper was ever found.'

Following the incident, the biggest shark hunt in Australia's history was launched. Dozens of innocent whites and whalers were killed, but none were large enough to have been the woman-eater. It was the first shark attack on a human ever in the Port Lincoln area, and one of the few where it has been proven that the victim was completely devoured. The tragedy and subsequent hunt were front page stories on all Australian newspapers for up to a week. The same weekend Shirley Anne Durden was killed, seven people died in South Australia alone, torn to pieces in road accidents. These terrible deaths hardly received any media coverage, though many of the victims suffered most horribly before dying. I am not putting down Mrs Durden's death, which, while horrifying, would have been painless and instantaneous, but trying to illustrate how a shark attack, possibly because of its rarity, but mainly I feel due to media over-dramatization, creates such a furore while equally tragic, but much more commonplace deaths cause little or no distress to the community as a whole.

It was South Australia's first shark fatality in over 10 years. Not a bad average for a state that is considered home of the Great White Death!

17
From *Sharks and Shipwrecks*

Hugh Edwards

Hugh Edwards has published many books about the sea. A journalist by profession, he is a diver by choice.

Sharks and Shipwrecks is a collection of true adventure stories involving the ocean. Hugh said that the idea came to him one day when he was thinking about different friends and the exciting lives they led. His thought was that they all had a story to tell, so he set off around Australia visiting all the people he had chosen for his book, writing down their tales. It is an interesting book, each story a personal account of adventure and experience.

'The Great Shark of Jurien Bay' is the story of Bob Bartle's fatal encounter with a great white. Every story of shark attack has its heroism. Bob's is no different.

He was a friend of ours, and, as an Australian would say, 'a real good bloke'. In those days all the active divers knew one another, so Bob's death was a terrible shock to us all.

Other friends have been attacked while spearfishing, but most have fought off the shark and survived. Bob never had that chance; he didn't see the shark before it attacked.

There are other stories in the book, including Ron's and mine. Ron talks of filming the great white and I, to be different, of my pet moray eels.

Sharks and Shipwrecks has been successful – it went on sale in the United States and Australia in 1975 and has been reprinted. It is a good true adventure book.

■

The Great Shark of Jurien Bay

A team of two, and a good team, they were the Western Australian State pairs spearfishing champions in 1967.

Bob was twenty-four, short but strongly built and with a pleasant manner which won friends easily. He was dedicated to diving and was the secretary of the Western Australian Council of Underwater Activities and an organizer to the Australian Spearfishing Championships, held at Busselton, Western Australia, in December 1967.

Lee was twenty-six. An ex-schoolteacher who made a living from diving for crayfish and from spearing fish. He had a tremendously powerful physique, very blue eyes, and a black bushy beard. He was the more brilliant diver of the two, but Bob had the best endurance and concentration. As a combination of strengths they were highly effective at their sport.

In August 1967, Bob Bartle and his bearded diving partner Lee Warner travelled the red dusty road to Jurien Bay 240 kilometres north of Perth in a Volkswagen with their spear guns.

They were going to compete in a spearfishing meeting. As competitions went, it was a minor one. But they regarded it as important. It was practice for them for the Australian Spearfishing Championships in four months' time.

In 1967, having learned hard lessons in gear and techniques in previous championships. Warner and Bartle had the national pairs title as their goal. On their home territory they knew they had a good chance of winning against divers from the Eastern States – provided they had a solid grounding of months of hard diving practice to build stamina and sharpen techniques.

So – though the cold and sullen winter waters of Jurien Bay were hardly inviting – they were looking forward to the meeting as a test of the progress they were making. Saturday, 19 August, was listed as a practice day – a chance for visiting divers to look over the ground and adapt their gear to local conditions. The actual competition, the fish spearing, would be held the next day, on Sunday the twentieth.

On the practice day Bob swung his Volkswagen off the track and braked to a halt on the high grey bluff of North Head at Jurien Bay, overlooking the area where the competition would be held.

He and Warner looked out over the reefs and breaking bomboras [submerged reefs] of the bay with practised eyes. The best ground looked to be a reef a mile or so offshore, and, with a few wry jokes about the weather, they got their gear out and began shrugging into their rubber wetsuits. Other divers from other cars were similarly getting into their gear, and they dressed quickly from long familiarity with their suits and equipment.

Lee had on a full-length neoprene rubber wetsuit to his ankles, while Bob's short suit went only to his knees. Both men wore close-fitting helmet hoods, and they carried the standard floats with diver's flags (red, with a white diagonal stripe) which they tow for identification and from which they would hang their speared fish from a wire toggle.

They walked down the bluff's steep slope to the water's edge, carrying their masks, flippers, lead belts, and big single-rubber spear guns, and after a quick look around, walked into the water, rinsed their masks and – with a grimace at the weather – began swimming.

They swam out from the grey limestone headland, heading for the deeper water about a mile offshore, looking for big fish like kingfish, groper, jewfish, as well as the smaller fish which counted for points in competition. They swam with the hard-kicking style of professionals, working hard to get warm and cover ground.

They had no thought of sharks, though both had seen plenty on the offshore reefs. Warner had kept himself in pocket money as a youth by shooting grey nurse and whalers for fish shops, and had had a brush or two with bigger sharks.

Bob had also been involved in shark accidents, like most of the deep reef spearfishermen, and had fought off a bronze whaler at Dunsborough in the south, jabbing it away with his loaded gun as it charged repeatedly.

After Dunsborough he had claimed, 'If anyone asks me if I'm scared of sharks I won't shrug my shoulders.'

Most sharks were regarded as summer fish, active when the seawater was warm. At Jurien that August, as they swam for the far-out reefs, they thought it would be too cold, much too cold, for sharks.

The bottom was weedy and featureless, until about 700 metres off the headland they came across a hole or depression in eight metres of water. It was about twelve metres across with overhanging ledges – the sort of place for jewfish.

'Might as well have a look,' Bob said.

Lee Warner nodded agreement. 'Right-o,' and Bob went down in a shallow glide, spear gun in front of him and dropping the lead sinker of his float line so it would not tangle as he swam through the caves under the ledges.

There were no jewfish. They prepared to move on, and Bob dived again for his float lead. He reached the bottom, picked it up, and as he was beginning to rise, Warner turned and began to swim on.

Suddenly an enormous black shape hurtled below Warner's flippers. It was a shark so big and moving so quickly that Warner – who had seen many sharks but nothing like this – gasped involuntarily.

Without slackening speed the shark hit Bartle, seizing him between shoulder and thigh, and striking with an impact which knocked his mask off. It began to shake him violently from side to side.

For an instant Warner remained frozen by the swiftness and unexpectedness of the attack. Instinct was to flee, but Lee was not lacking in courage.

He had killed sharks before, though nothing of this size. But he knew that a spear in the tiny brain could immobilize even a giant.

Warner dived down towards the struggling shapes on the bottom, aiming his spear gun as he dived.

'I went straight down and put a spear in the top of the shark's head right where I figured the brain should be. It hit with a solid clunk. But it didn't seem to affect it, except that it attracted the brute's attention to me. It sort of shook its head, then bit Bob in half and rose up at me...'

The shark swam upward through a cloud of blood, the lower part of Bob still in its jaws, flippers protruding.

'Christ!' said Warner to himself, eyes bulging in horror behind the mask.

As it came at him he pushed himself away from it with the unloaded gun, jabbing at the great black eye with the butt. The eye rolled white. 'I didn't think sharks could do that.' His mind was curiously detached for a moment. But he was soon brought back to reality.

'Never in my life have I seen anything so chilling than watching that shark circling around me with the body of Bob still in its jaws. From less than one metre I could see the terrible wounds inflicted. I was helpless. I could see Bob was dead. That was only too obvious. I thought I was soon to follow. I simply cannot describe the terror which flowed through me...'

The water was now dark with blood and shapes were distorted and indistinct – grotesque in the twilight of darkened water. The enormous shadow moved through it all.

'It kept circling about eight feet from me. Its body looked about five feet thick from top to bottom. I didn't really get a good idea of its length – I couldn't see the extremities and don't remember seeing the tail. All I could see was the eye and what it had in its mouth.'

He had a moment of mesmerised indecision.

'Then out of the corner of my eye I saw Bob's gun which was still loaded and floating just below the surface. I grabbed it gratefully, and swinging it around tried to belt the spear into the shark's eye. But the eye was set close to the top of its head and somehow the spear just whistled harmlessly over the top of its head. It was the worst shot of my life. I don't know how I could have missed, and I've cursed myself for it a thousand times since.

'That was my last real chance to get back at the shark.

'It kept swimming round and round and started getting caught and tangled up in all the lines. It was tied to my gun by the line from the first spear and my gun picked up the float lines. There was just one big tangled mess. I was scared of getting caught up in the lines myself.

'The shark was black on top and white on its guts. A sort of mottled pattern. It looked weird in the bad winter light and the blood-reddened water. I could see its jaw was much wider than the body – the jaw must have been a metre wide at least. Maybe more.

'I knew Bob was dead. And there was the thought of other sharks.

'A little bronze whaler came and began darting around in the blood. Were there any more big ones? I swam backwards, fast. From 100 yards away I looked back and saw the shark still moving around tangled in the lines and floats on the same spot.

'I felt pretty bloody helpless, I can tell you. But once I lost sight of it I began free-styling for shore. It wasn't too far but it seemed miles. Now and again I looked back to convince myself the shark was still back there. I was still frightened.

'I swam away from a friend and diving companion of seven years, and that's something I'll never forget. Not as long as I live.'

Warner reached the shallows and ran from the water stumbling. When he looked back he could see one or two flags and floats of other divers far out at sea, unaware of the tragedy that had taken place so close to them. It all seemed unreal – in fact the sense of nightmarish unreality never left him.

He searched for the keys to Bob's Volkswagen, parked up on top of the bluff at North Head, and couldn't find them. But he found a key to one of the other cars and drove, skidding around the corners, ten kilometres along the dirt track to Sandy Cape, a crayfishing settlement, to gasp out his story and ask for a boat to get the other divers out of the water.

The season was over, but one or two boats still swung on the moorings with silent engines. Harry Holme's *Gar Fan* was one, a thirteen-and-a-half-metre steel boat. Harry agreed at once to go to North Head and in a short time they were off the grey headland, with the cray boat rolling in the winter swell.

They could see the two divers' floats and the tangle of lines, and something dark below them. The shark was still there.

There was something else floating too. A human torso cut through across the breastbone by the teeth of the giant shark.

Bob still had air in his lungs. Death must have been very quick, for he had not even cried out. It may be that he was never aware of what had happened, and his diving friends have always hoped so.

When they took hold of the tangled lines in the hope they might catch the beast, the shark – that vast, indistinct shape on the bottom – began to swim slowly away. It was incredibly strong. The cords snapped one by one. The metal fittings on the spears straightened out. Then it was gone.

The divers went back to Jurien Bay and held a wake that night. Next day they held their spearfishing competition as it had been planned. It wasn't bravado, and it was something other than plain courage.

'Bob would have wanted it that way,' they said.

A massive hunt was launched for the shark and rewards were offered for its capture. But it was never seen again.

No one was quite sure even what kind of shark it was. It is a measure of the horror of that day that Warner – normally a meticulous observer of marine life – was unable to remember clearly anything about it except the great dark eyes and what it had in its mouth.

The argument has never been resolved about whether it was a huge tiger, black-backed with age, or that known killer and maimer of divers, the great white shark.

The presence of breeding seals on nearby islands might explain the attack. The shark – like the one which attacked Henri Bource in Victoria three years earlier – may have mistaken Bob Bartle for a seal. But why did it pass under Lee Warner's flippers to attack the man on the seabed? That is a question which still occasionally faces Warner in his nightmares.

At Jurien Bay today there stands a simple memorial to Bob Bartle.

18
From *Shark Attack*

H. David Baldridge

H. David Baldridge's book *Shark Attack* is the most up-to-date, comprehensive collection of shark attack accounts available to the general public that I know of.

The case histories cited in this book have been collected from all over the world, and the information studied with the aid of a computer.

Baldridge was director of the United States Navy International Shark Attack File. This file was compiled with the aid of the marine division of the Smithsonian Institution.

They studied 1,652 cases which contained sufficient information to be of use to the computer study. Of these, Baldridge chose about two hundred for the book.

Shark Attack also contains a good deal of other interesting scientific information about sharks of all species. A few lines that appear in the middle of page 223 (not from this selection) are so true, yet the opposite to common belief, that I must repeat them here.

Baldridge writes: 'Only about one-fourth of all attack victims received wounds of a nature and number to suggest that hunger might have provoked the attack. Sharks repeatedly strike their victim in a wild, frenzied fashion only about 4% of the time.'

All our experience with sharks has shown that they are not man-eaters in the true sense of the word, and it is gratifying to find an expert of the calibre of Baldridge agreeing with our observations.

Shark Attack, although a collection of facts about a serious scientific study, has been written in a simple easy style that makes enjoyable reading. It is having a success with the public not usually associated with scientific publication.

The following excerpt is typical of the honest and to-the-point manner in which Baldridge has presented the information he compiled.

■

Approximately two-thirds of all documented shark attacks have occurred since 1940. The average of about 28 cases per year is far below the estimate of 100 often stated in scientific and popular literature as the world-wide yearly incidence of shark attack. Keep in mind that the likelihood of an attack being reported would surely depend upon the degree of injury received by the victim. Fatalities are usually given widespread publicity, and, except for some wartime cases and those happening in the most remote regions of the world, accounts of attacks in recent years resulting in death to the victims would very likely be on file.

The peak year for attacks in modern times was reached with 56 cases reported in 1959. It is probably more than a coincidence that the Shark Research Panel was established in 1958 and that a great amount of effort was devoted shortly thereafter to building up the SAF (Shark Attack File). It seems reasonable that the attendant publicity would have produced a sharp increase in efficiency of reporting attacks. On the other hand, there is also the possibility that we actually have been enjoying since 1959 a period of decreasing incidence of shark attack for which there is no ready explanation. During the period 1941–1958, reported attacks increased at an average rate of about 1.2 cases per year. But since the peak year of 1959, known attacks have fallen off at the approximate rate of 2.0 cases per year, with only about 23 expected for 1973.

Mortality rates have generally decreased (dropping an average of about 1 per cent per year) from 46 per cent in 1940 to an estimated 16 per cent for 1973, with an overall mortality rate of 35 per cent for the SAF as a whole. The general decline in death rates could be due to a number of factors, the most obvious of which would be a steady rise in the availability to attack victims of early, more advanced medical attention. Another important factor could be that continuing improvements in worldwide communications have led to the reporting of ever-increasing percentages of attacks involving non-fatal injuries.

There is no evidence at all to link incidence of shark attack with gross variations in shark populations or general turns by sharks towards more or less aggressive behaviour. Instead, attack rates are more likely related to the ballooning human population and the extent to which people make themselves available for attack by their use of the sea for recreational purposes.

Now, if the incidence of shark attack is truly strongly dependent upon the number of people exposed to attack at any particular time, then it would be expected that attacks would happen more often at those times when people are more likely to frequent beaches in large numbers. It took my son, David, to point out that weekends should provide the greater opportunity for encounters between bathers and sharks. Of those cases which have occurred since 1900, 729 could be identified as to day of the week. We found on the average that about 65 per cent more attacks occurred on days of the weekend than on weekdays, strongly supporting the contention that shark attack was, and presumably still is, more likely to occur at those times when the greater numbers of people are in the water.

As I will do from time to time, let me add a word of caution in regard to interpretation of these data. Because of the total lack of consideration of control information, the above observation does not in any way point to Saturday and Sunday as being the most dangerous days to plan a beach outing. Nor is it necessarily implied that the danger is greater to any particular individual when many people are in the water. To evaluate the relative hazard potential as it would affect individuals would require detailed knowledge of beach populations (people actually in the water) both on uneventful days and those associated directly with attacks. This sort of information is not available.

Now, how about the time of day as related to total numbers of attacks? There is a steady rise in attack rate beginning in early morning to peak around 11:00 A.M, falling off markedly around noon, followed by a rise to a larger peak at midafternoon, and finally falling again to very low numbers at about nightfall. Our own experiences tell us that this pattern of activity is consistent with the way in which people in general make use of the waters at beaches. The population builds up during the morning hours followed by at least a partial withdrawal from the water about lunchtime. The afternoon brings with it more people and sends some of the noon picnickers back into the water. As dusk approaches, the peak afternoon crowd heads for home. Direct confirmation of this impression of human habit patterns was provided by my colleague, Edward Broedel, who actually counted people (a total of 1,018) in the water, hour by hour, on a day of heavy attendance at Brytle Beach, South Carolina.

Here again, taken out of context and without consideration of control data, the high incidence of shark attack during the afternoon hours could lead one to conclude that for an individual swimming at a beach, the greatest chance of encountering an aggressive shark would be during the midafternoon. The data in no way support this, for to evaluate the relative danger facing any particular individual as a function of time of day would require knowledge of numbers of people exposed but not attacked, hour by hour, and on a worldwide basis information that would be essentially impossible to obtain. Yet, the hourly pattern of attack does point to a very important fact, especially when considered along with the finding of higher incidence of shark attack on weekends. Both observations indicate that the rate of attack is strongly associated with the numbers of people in the water.

With these findings in mind, it seems reasonable to assume that shark attack can occur at any time in waters where populations of sharks (including a population of one) can come into contact with man. On a long time basis, the incidence of attacks would be strongly related to those periods of time when potential victims are more abundant. Even though lack of control data prevents any inference concerning danger to a particular individual swimmer, the chance of at least some unspecified person being attacked at any particular beach would be expected to increase as the concentration of people in the water increases. The time periods for such correlations are long, and the above considerations do not in any way deny the possibility of short-term rashes of attacks at times of low beach population. Neither do they mitigate against periods of calm even though the beaches are flooded with people. Such is the way it is with statistics.

All but four reported attacks have occurred between latitudes of 47 degrees South and 46 degrees North. The exceptions all involved injuries inflicted upon fishermen by captured sharks and were thus considered to have been provoked. The most northerly was probably that on Hans Schapper (Case 770) who, in June 1960, was bitten on the right arm by a small shark that had been inadvertently brought aboard a trawler in a fish-laden net. Although the victim was treated at Wick, Scotland, the exact geographical location of the accident was not reported. Another northerly provoked attack happened on 4 August 1960 off the South Devon coast in the English Channel not far from Dartmouth, England, when William Chapel (Case 786) had his arm sliced open from elbow to wrist as he was pulling on board an 80-pound shark that had been hooked by an angler.

The most northerly unprovoked attacks occurred not in oceanic waters, but in upper reaches of the Adriatic Sea near the Istria peninsula of Yugoslavia. Unfortunately, information about them is very skimpy. On 4 September 1934, eighteen-year-old Agnes Novak was fatally injured near Susak (Case 370). The London *Times* reported in July 1954 that a Hungarian refugee and a companion set out to swim from Pola (Pula) towards Fiume (Rijeka), and only one reached safety, the other being taken by a shark (Case 309). Seven years later, in September 1961, Sabi Plana, a nineteen-year-old student, was swimming about 75 yards from shore with seven other students near the Adriatic Sea resort of Opatija. A large shark surfaced, bit off his left hand and injured his legs. The boy died before a boat from shore could reach him (Case 946).

From those Adriatic waters also came the strange tale of Zorca Prince (Case 974). On 30 August 1934, the New York *Evening Sun* carried a story datelined Fiume, Yugoslavia. It told of a young girl who paid with her life because she did not believe in dreams. Her mother had pleaded with her in a letter not to swim far from shore, for she had had a dream that Zorca would fall victim to a shark. Exclaiming to her friends, 'I don't believe in dreams,' the young student, a strong swimmer, made for a fishing boat far out in the sea off Reotore. The fishermen heard a shriek and went to help the girl only to find nothing but bloodstained water. They reported that a shark had been seen earlier swimming around the edge of their nets. But for a followup article in another newspaper a few days later, the case would have gone on record as a bonafide fatal shark attack. With a dateline of Belgrade, 1 September, the second article read, 'It is reported from Kraljevica in the Alvala District that the news published by certain foreign papers according to which a young Yugoslavian girl, Miss Prinz, was attacked and eaten by a shark off the Italian coast, is without foundation. Miss Prinz is actually at her parents' home in Ljubljana and intends to spend the coming month taking examinations for admission to the university of this town.' So, fortunately for Zorca Prince, we have replaced the red fatality tag on our File 974 with a green one indicating serious doubt that anything at all happened, It remains, however, one of numerous examples of how quickly and with essentially no actual evidence people are willing to accept a tale of shark attack.

The most southerly shark attacks have occurred off South Island, New Zealand, almost directly opposite the Adriatic Sea on the surface of the earth. Only one attack has been reported from below the 46th Parallel, and this one was relatively minor. Norman McEwan, on 27 January 1962, received small but deep gashes on his wrist when he was seized by a 5-foot shark while swimming in waist-deep water off Oreti Beach at the southern end of South Island (Case 1088). Several very appalling attacks have occurred below the 45th Parallel in the waters off South Island. In the early years of this century, a Mr Grant was floating on his back in the open sea near Oamaru when a shark grabbed him by the arm (Case 924) injuring it severely enough to cause loss by amputation. At about the same period of time near Moeraki, a Dunedin businessman, W. M. Hutchinson, was standing in water up to his waist, while his son was playing by diving off his shoulders. The boy had dived twice and was getting ready for a third dive, when a shark suddenly bit right through the man's leg, mortally wounding him (Case 925). Three more fatal attacks have occurred off South Island in more recent years.

At approximately 7:00 A.M. on the morning of 5 February 1964, Leslie Jordan was enjoying his usual morning swim in the chilly (58° F) surf at St Clair Beach, Dunedin (Case 1266). After swimming some 250 yards into the sea, he suddenly began to wave his arms wildly and cry for help. A man on a paddleboard about 50 yards away went to his assistance, thinking that Jordan had suffered a cramp. As the paddler pulled alongside, the swimmer said he had been attacked by a shark and raised a leg to show massive wounds that were by now deeply staining the water. Jordan half crawled and was half pulled across the paddleboard, with his legs still in the water from midthigh downward. The rescuer gave the raised-arm signal for assistance. Shortly before a second paddler arrived, the shark was seen at the surface near the board, its dorsal fin and tail out of the water, a foot or two longer than the 10-foot paddleboard. The victim was unconscious by the time the second board came alongside and was then pulled completely from the water across both boards. As they neared the shore, a breaking wave tossed them all into the surf. The two men carried Jordan to the beach and immediately commenced resuscitation. It was only then that they realized the extent of his wounds. The right leg had been amputated through the knee joint. Behind the leg just above the knee joint there was a gaping wound, the edge of which showed four teeth marks. There was also a grazing mark six inches long and three inches wide on the inner side of the left leg made possibly by the shark's fins. The inside calf of the left leg was deeply lacerated with what appeared to be tooth marks above and below the wound. There were also other small lacerations on the thigh of the left leg from the knee to the buttock. All efforts failed to elicit any sign of life, and the victim never regained consciousness. Later postmortem findings indicated that he had become unconscious from loss of blood and shock while being brought in, and in that state had inhaled a quantity of water leading to death by drowning. The first rescuer testified that the victim's right leg had been intact, with the exception of a piece missing from the thigh, when he first approached Jordan. He concluded that the shark must have made a second attack, taking the lower right leg, as they awaited arrival of the second paddler. All evidence indicated the attacker to have been a great white shark, 10 to 12 feet in length.

As it has happened in other places, the respite from shark attack that South Island had enjoyed for so many years prior to the attack on Jordan was again broken a few years later when William Black was taken by a shark at St Kilda Beach, Dunedin, on 9 March 1967 (Case 1449). The water was murky and cold (55–57° F). A light rain was falling. The time was 7:15 P.M., a few minutes after sunset. Black was taking part in a belt race with a fellow life-saving club member and was leading his opponent by about 20 yards. Suddenly, a large shark appeared and the water around Black quickly turned dark with blood. Those on shore also saw the shark's fin and commenced to pull in the lines attached to belts worn by the swimmers. Black's line suddenly went slack and was reeled in quickly. The line was found to be severed, with the belt and Black missing. A surf canoe was launched, but the search was fruitless and had to be abandoned as darkness fell. Subsequent intensive searches failed to uncover any trace of the missing swimmer.

The line separating tragedy from good fortune is sometimes very thin indeed. And so it was for seventeen-year-old Gary Barton (Case

1583) on Christmas Day in 1968 at St Clair Beach, Dunedin. It was at this beach that Leslie Jordan lost his life to a shark almost four years earlier. Barton was riding a surfboard in 59-degree water about 50 yards from the beach when he saw something of 'whitey browny colour with a black nose' in the water beneath him. Suddenly he was knocked from the board and left hanging on to it by his arms. He quickly drew himself back aboard and lay flat on his stomach. But then the shark rose from the water, hitting Barton in the face with its snout, knocking him back into the water. As chance would have it, the shark did not press its advantage, and Barton was able to climb back onto his surfboard and paddle safely to shore. The fibreglass board didn't fare so well, for it bore on each of its sides a set of tooth marks up to one-inch deep along with a deep gash some 5 inches long.

The chain of attacks off South Island was to continue, for on 15 September 1968, in 55-degree waters only about 30 yards off the entrance to Otago Harbor, a 14-foot great white shark fatally mauled a twenty-four-year-old spearfisherman, Graham Hitt (Case 1550). One of a group of five skin divers, Hitt, clad in a full black wetsuit, had been spearing fish some 100 yards from the seaward end of a jetty in relatively clear water which dropped off rapidly to a depth of about 50 feet. One of the divers was startled by a very large shark with an eye 'as large as a baseball' as it suddenly swam past him at a range of about 8 feet. The shark left his field of view but quickly returned, appearing to be moving in an agitated manner, balancing and pivoting on the tips of its pectoral fins which were about 6 to 8 feet apart. Just as the shark seemed to the diver to be positioning itself for a strike, it heeled over and made directly for Hitt, who was then swimming at the surface in a horizontal position and not facing the shark as it attacked. In a tremendous flurry of foaming water, the shark grabbed Hitt, shook him, just as suddenly let him go, and, after making one more circuit, turned and swam away. His companions courageously responded to Hitt's cries for help, moving quickly to his side and bringing him into shore. But death had been quick; there being no sign of life by the time they reached safety. In apparently a single bite, the shark had cut through the left leg to the bone, severing the femoral and other adjacent arteries. There were also a few tooth marks on the right leg. Pathologists later removed several tooth fragments from grooves in the left femur, the largest of which was 28.7 millimetres long and clearly identified the attacker as a great white shark. It is interesting to note that the shark showed no apparent interest in floats, only 10 to 15 yards away, which held several previously speared fish. One official advanced the theory that the shark could have mistaken the shiny black suit of the diver for one of the seals which are common in the area.

Even though the above attacks occurred at the most extreme latitudes, both north and south, it should not be taken that they also were necessarily the ones associated with the lowest water temperatures.

The Southern Hemisphere has only a slight edge, 54 per cent in the total numbers of reported and coded shark attacks. The distributions within each hemisphere follow the same general patterns, i.e. very few attacks near the equator, rising to a peak at the middle latitudes, and falling off rapidly at higher latitudes. Although I have no actual data to support it, this pattern of attacks versus latitude generally follows what I would expect in terms of worldwide population distribution. Here again, it appears as if the availability of people rather than sharks may determine the incidence of shark attack, considering the probable omnipresence of sharks in general in waters between latitudes 46° N and 47° S....

The heavy predominance of attacks reported from English-speaking countries is highly suggestive of a language barrier in the procedures for gathering information on such happenings in other localities. There seems to be a particular lack of communication with Latin countries, especially those in Central and South America from which only a total of 25 cases are held in the SAF.

19

From *About Sharks and Shark Attacks*

David H. Davies

Dr Davies was the director of the Oceanographic Research Institute and Aquarium in Durban, South Africa. He was considered a world authority on sharks and their behaviour. His book *About Sharks and Shark Attack* is based on the sharks that infest the waters surrounding South Africa. It is well illustrated with excellent photographs (some of them quite gruesome) and drawings.

Throughout his book Dr Davies is extremely thorough, but often the correct information regarding the attack is confused and incomplete. This is understandable, for at such a time neither victim nor bystander are carefully filing away everything they see for scientific use. Often in the horror and panic of an attack, little, if anything, is remembered about what actually took place. The picture that emerges at a later date, while the best available, may not be anything like the correct one.

The piece that I have chosen from the book covers an attack which is an exception. The attack on Michael Hely is one of the best documented reports of a shark attack that I have ever read.

Dr Davies managed to record the entire incident, and all the particulars related to it, in fine detail. The report of the medical procedures used has value for everyone who could conceivably be involved in a shark attack, sailors, divers and surfers alike.

At first, the ragged tooth shark (in Australia, the grey nurse) was blamed for the attack. It was not until a more detailed examination of the wounds and teeth fragments were made that the true culprit, the Zambesi shark, was identified.

This is a fair indication that many sharks are attributed to the wrong species and that all shark attack identifications are suspect. Many species look similar, making positive identification by nonexperts difficult, especially when the only sight of the fish is in the water during the confusion and panic of the actual attack.

■

Shark Attack on Michael Hely

Michael Hely, a European male aged sixteen years was swimming in slightly murky water at Inyoni Rocks near Amanzimototi at 3:35 P.M.

on 30 April 1960. The temperature of the water was 71° F (21° C). Michael, who was a bricklayer's apprentice at the time, was wearing a pair of home-made swimming trunks, coloured yellow and red, and he wore a silver ring on a finger of his right hand. The colour of his skin was light tan.

He swam into a channel in the surf zone approximately 10 feet deep and 30 feet from the shore and was 'treading water' when he felt something touch his right leg. He thought that he had brushed against a stick or some other submerged object. Immediately afterwards he felt pressure and a downward pull on his right arm and was dragged below the surface of the water. At that moment, he realized that he was being attacked by a shark and he began a desperate fight for his life. He recalled a frenzied underwater struggle with his assailant lasting a few seconds; he broke free and on coming to the surface began to swim towards the shore when he was again attacked and was bitten on the right side. The shark remained at his side during his swim to the shore. On reaching the shore, Michael staggered out unaided. It is interesting to note that up to this time he had not felt any sensation of pain.

He was carried to the Life Saver's Office and was attended within twelve minutes by a doctor from Amanzimototi who found that his injuries were serious and that he was in a shocked condition.

Michael's injuries included bite wounds on the right leg, the right forearm and hand, a finger of the left hand, and a very extensive wound on the right flank with widespread removal of skin and the lateral abdominal wall. This resulted in exposure and perforation of the large and small bowel, exposure of the right kidney and the hip bone (the entire iliac crest), and the removal of most of the right gluteal muscles.

In spite of severe loss of blood and the extent of his injuries, he remained conscious, was given morphine, and was placed in a head-down position to ensure a good supply of blood to the brain. He responded well to this treatment and was quiet and rational when taken to the Addington Hospital in Durban – a journey of 15 miles which took 45 minutes.

An investigation of the bacteriology of the victim's wounds in the arm and leg was carried out and the same haemolytic paracolon bacillus was isolated that had been found on the teeth and in the mouths of living sharks as a result of a bacteriological investigation carried out previously by the Oceanographic Research Institute in collaboration with medical research associates. Infection by this organism could result in the death of a victim, but an effective antibiotic treatment had previously been devised and is now administered as a routine to shark attack victims.

Four months after the attack, all the wounds had healed extremely well without the need for skin grafting even for the extensive abdominal injury.

There is little doubt that Michael Hely owes his life to the effective emergency treatment he received on the beach and the very considerable ability of the surgeons of the Addington Hospital.

The case of Michael Hely was the first investigated by the Oceanographic Research Institute and at the time the species of shark found off the coast of Natal were not fully known.

Thorough investigation of the wounds revealed no fragments of shark's teeth and it was necessary to carry out a careful evaluation of the characteristics of the victim's wounds in order to try and find out what species of shark had been responsible for the attack.

The findings of a retrospective study of this kind can naturally never be stated with complete certainty and, in fact, led to the tentative conclusion at the time that the shark responsible was a ragged tooth shark, *Carcharhinus taurus.*

This conclusion was to a large extent based on the presence of bony lesions in the hip bone of the victim caused by the teeth of the shark. These consisted of two narrow grooves as deep as 3 centimetres in the iliac crest. Although the characteristics of the other wounds did not necessarily support this conclusion, it did not seem possible that any teeth other than the long, nonserrated, stilettolike teeth of the ragged tooth shark could have caused lesions of this type.

A subsequent investigation of the characteristics of Michael Hely's wounds, using the extensive photographic records together with measurements and other data collected at the time of the attack, has shown that the characteristics of the wounds conform to those found subsequently to have been caused by the Zambezi shark, *Carcharhinus leucas,* which has flattened, triangular teeth with serrated edges.

The leg wounds consist of rows of small lesions triangular in shape while the edges of the extensive abdominal injury are generally clean cut as in all bites from Zambezi sharks, rather than torn (the ragged tooth sharks are of the tearing type). An explanation for the deep grooves in the iliac crest can be found in the suggestion that the flat cutting teeth of the attacking shark swept edge-on across the bone, producing narrow grooves rather than shearing off the entire iliac crest. Some indication of the size of the shark may be obtained from the size of the sweep of the jaws as shown in the tooth marks on the right leg. Reference to the extensive collection of prepared specimens of jaws in the Oceanographic Research Institute suggests that the shark was probably about 7 feet in length and weighed in the vicinity of 200 pounds.

20

From *Shark Attack*

Victor M. Coppleson

Shark Attack is a vivid account of a predatory white shark which makes *Jaws* seem even more possible. Again, fact is stranger than fiction.

It is interesting that both Rodney Fox and Brian Rogers were attacked during spearfishing competitions at Aldinga Beach. Sixteen-year-old Jeff Corner was fatally attacked at Cardcalinga, twenty-two kilometres south of Aldinga, also during a spearfishing competition. The attacks were over three consecutive years, but there is a definite possibility that the same shark could have been responsible for all three attacks.

This series of attacks, in fact, fits Sir Victor Coppleson's 'rogue shark' theory, which appears again and again in the different attacks described in his book.

So little is known about sharks. Some research has been done on the more harmless species, but the larger and better armed a shark is, the less scientists seem inclined to study it.

Many big-game fishermen feel that the great white shark has a territory which he patrols. Just how big the territory is is anyone's guess. It could take days, weeks, or even months for a single shark to complete the circuit of its particular territory, which could explain the differing intervals between attacks in related areas.

This is only a theory based on the observations of a few shark fishermen, but, with regard to the great white shark, it is the best information available.

Coppleson's book documents shark attacks from all over the world and presents a massive amount of evidence to support his arguments. He divided the attacks into localities, types of attack, methods of defence, and repellents. The mass of information Coppleson collected was first printed in 1958 and, at the time, was one of the best documented publications on sharks and their behaviour in relation to man.

■

This theory of cruising rogue sharks attacking over long distances might well have been flimsy, were it not for a series of attacks which occurred in July 1916 over a stretch of more than 60 miles of coastline along the eastern seaboard of the United States. It is hard to dismiss the claim that these were all the work of one killer and to the theorist they are the classic example of the activity of a long-range cruising rogue.

So serious were the incidents associated with the attacks that the entire United States was shocked and the matter was discussed by President Wilson and his cabinet. What the cabinet considered was one of the most remarkable series of shark attacks in world history. In ten days, attacks occurred along 65 miles of the Atlantic coast just below New York, killing four and injuring another.

At the time, it was generally believed in the United States that sharks were harmless. So strong was the disinclination to believe they could be man-killers that after the first attack, an authority, Dr F. A. Lucas, said publicly that there was little danger of a shark attacking anyone. The facts of the attack were examined, and five days later Dr Lucas retracted this statement.

The series of attacks by what was described as the 'mad shark' began on 2 July 1916 at Beach Haven, New Jersey, a popular summer resort, about 70 miles south of New York and not far from Atlantic City.

A twenty-four-old man named Vansant was swimming in about 5 feet of water at 5:00 P.M. There were only a few others with him. The nearest was about 40 feet away. Sheridan Taylor saw Vansant standing alone shoulder deep in the sea. He heard Vansant scream and saw him wildly beat the water. Taylor was almost immobilized for a second. Then he saw the water turn red and rushed towards Vansant. Taylor saw the shark clearly. Its fin and part of its back were well out of the water. Taylor grabbed Vansant and with the aid of others, who formed a human chain, began pulling him in. The shark came too, its jaws on its victim's leg.

Taylor could have touched it without any effort. They came right in until they stood in about 18 inches of water. The shark was still there. Then it turned and made off. On the sand a medical student applied a tourniquet above severe injuries on the man's left leg, but Vansant died a few hours after reaching hospital. This killer, observers said later, was bluish-grey and about 10 feet long.

On 6 July, four days later, Charles Bruder lost his life in a similar manner at Spring Lake, 35 miles farther north. His right leg was taken off just below the knee and the left leg amputated by the shark's teeth at the ankle. They were horrible injuries, and Bruder died a few minutes after being rescued.

Hundreds of men and women and many children were on the beach on the afternoon when Bruder, far out beyond the outer life lines, raised a cry for help. Two lifeguards, George White and Chris

Anderson, who had been watching the swimmer closely because of his distance from the shore, launched a lifeboat and started for Bruder while the crowd on the beach watched. As the lifeguards drew near, the water about Bruder was suddenly tinged with red. When White and Anderson reached Bruder, he cried out that a shark had bitten him. He then fainted.

On the beach an attempt was made to bandage his wounds while a doctor was called. Before one arrived, Bruder was dead.

This second attack horrified people in the area. Motorboat patrols were instituted in a number of resorts. Wire-netting enclosures were set up. The entire coastal area went into a kind of systematic and organized panic.

Bruder's death renewed the controversy that had raged for years as to whether a shark would attack a man. It was suggested at the time that a turtle or huge mackerel had killed him. In support of that theory it was pointed out that the victim's legs were torn and chewed as though something had hacked them, and not bitten with the clean, sharp bite supposed to be characteristic of shark. Colonel W. G. Schauffler, Surgeon-General of the National Guard of New Jersey, and a member of Governor Fielder's staff, who attended Bruder just before his death, described the wounds on the young man's body. Because of the question raised by some as to whether or not Bruder had really been attacked by a shark, Colonel Schauffler's description of the wounds is detailed.

Bruder's right leg, he said, had been taken off so that the bone stuck out to a point halfway between the knee and the ankle. The foot and ankle had been bitten off and were missing. The flesh was ripped as high as the knee, and the bone was denuded of flesh. The left leg had been bitten off at the ankle, the lower ends of the two leg bones protruding from the flesh fully one-third of the length of the leg. There was a very deep circular gash above the left knee, extending down to the bone. On the right side of the abdomen a piece of flesh had been gouged out.

After the attack at Spring Lake, experienced surf men and fishermen ridiculed the elaborate precautions taken, asserting that sharks had never been sighted although some small blue-nosed sharks had been caught near the fish pounds at Asbury.

On the other hand, a shark fisherman, T. Hermann Berringer, Jr., said he believed the increase in the number of fish pounds had attracted more sharks to the area.

This fatality caused the *New York Times*, in an editorial, to say:

If the 500 dollars offered some 25 years ago, by Hermann Oelrichs, for proof of an attack by a shark on a living man, were still to be won, claims for it apparently more than plausible would now be coming in from Spring Lake, down on the Jersey coast. To be sure the accounts from there now at hand do not include the statement of any witness who saw a shark ... and tales of exciting happenings off beach resorts are commonly to be accepted with caution. This tale, however, for a time at least, will considerably reduce the profits of a not-too-prosperous season. It certainly was not invented for advertising purposes and unless it was a shark that took off Bruder's leg, what could it have been? ... a reckless imagination might suggest the propeller of a German submarine...

Two days after the attack, Captain Frank Claret of the liner *Minnehaha* made a statement. He was astounded, he said, that man-eating sharks had been seen at Jersey beaches. It was the first time he had ever known man-eaters to go north of the Bahamas.

'The best thing to do if a shark comes at you,' said Captain Claret, 'is to shout as loud as you can and splash the water with your hands and feet.' (It might be noted here that the effectiveness of such advice depends entirely on the disposition of the particular shark.)

Reports from incoming steamers supported a theory that man-eaters along the Jersey coast had been driven north by hunger. Skipper of the vessel *Atlantic* (Captain Brewer) said he had seen sharks swimming northward. Off Cape Hatteras his steamer had passed the largest school of sharks he had ever seen. Some were huge monsters.

After the attacks were investigated, Dr. J. T. Nichols, Curator of the Department of Fisheries of the American Museum of Natural History, retracted a statement he made on 8 July that there was very little danger of a shark attacking anyone.

Of course – it happens everywhere – bathers quickly forgot about sharks. Then on 12 July the nation was galvanized. The rogue shark cycle was completed. On that day a ten-year-old boy and a young man were torn to death by the ravages of a shark. Another youngster was torn from hip to knee by the same monster. It was this third and final tragedy that shook the nation and caused President Wilson to summon his cabinet to consider the menace.

Early on 12 July, Captain Thomas Cottrell, a retired mariner, saw a dark grey shape swimming in the shallow waters of Matawan Creek. The creek was only 30 miles by sea north of Spring Lake, but it was 20 miles from the ocean. Captain Cottrell recalled the two swimmers killed by sharks on the New Jersey coast. He hurried to town and spread the warning among the two thousand residents that a shark had entered Matawan Creek.

Everywhere they laughed at him. How could a shark get 20 miles away from the ocean, swim through Raritan Bay, and enter the shallow creek? Thus the townfolk reasoned, and grownups and children flocked to the creek as usual for their daily dip.

But Captain Cottrell was right. That night a body lay in the Long Branch Memorial Hospital. A dead child lay somewhere in the dark water and in St Peter's Hospital, New Brunswick, doctors worked throughout the night maintaining the life of another lad torn about the hip.

It was unfortunate that the first victim, ten-year-old Lester Stilwell suffered from fits. When he was convulsed in the water and went below the surface, Stanley Fisher, son of the retired commodore of the Savannah Line, assumed the boy had taken a fit and raced to the centre of the creek to his aid. Young Stilwell came to the surface as Fisher approached. The lad screamed and yelled and waved his arms wildly. His body swirled round and round in the water. Fisher was warned it might be a shark. 'A shark here?' he said incredulously. 'I don't care, anyway. I'm going after that boy.'

When he got to the centre of the stream there was no sign of the lad. Fisher dived once, twice. At last he came up with the bloodstained figure in his arms.

He was nearer the opposite shore and struck out in that direction while Arthur Smith and Joseph Deulew put out in a motorboat to bring him back. Fisher was almost on the shore. When his feet touched the bottom, the onlookers heard him utter a cry and saw him throw up his arms. Stilwell's body slipped back into the stream. With another cry, Fisher was dragged after it.

'The shark! The shark!' cried the crowd ashore, and other men sprang into motorboats and started for the spot where Fisher had disappeared. Smith and Deulew were in the lead, but before they overtook him Fisher had risen and dragged himself to the bank where he collapsed.

Those who reached him found the young man's right leg stripped of flesh from above the hip at the waist line to a point below the knee. He was senseless from shock and pain, but was resuscitated by Dr. G. L. Reynolds after Recorder Arthur Van Buskirk had made a tourniquet of rope and staunched the flow of blood from Fisher's frightful wounds.

Fisher said he was in less than three or four feet of water when the shark grabbed him, and he had had no notion of sharks until that instant. If he had thought of them at all, he said, he had felt himself safe when he got his feet on the bottom. He had felt the nip on his leg, and looking down, had seen the shark clinging to him. Others ashore said they saw the white belly of the shark as it turned to seize him. Fisher was carried across the river and hurried by train to the hospital at Long Branch. He died before he could be carried to the operating table.

At the creek, meantime, dynamite had been procured. Arrangements were being made to detonate it off, when a motorboat raced up to the steamboat pier. At the wheel was J. R. Lefferts. In the craft lay twelve-year-old John Dunn. With his brother William and several others, he had been swimming off the New Jersey spot when Stilwell and Fisher were attacked.

News of the accident had reached the boys and they had hurried from the water. Dunn was the last to leave, and as he drew himself up on the brick company's pier, with his left leg trailing in the water, the shark struck. Its teeth shut over the leg above and below the knee and much of the flesh had been torn away. He was taken to a factory nearby, where Dr H. J. Cooley, of Keyport, dressed his wounds, and then by car to St Peter's Hospital, New Brunswick, where the torn leg was amputated. Two days later they found Lester Stilwell's body resting against the shore 100 yards upstream from the place where he was attacked. There were seven wounds, four on the body, two on the left leg, and one on the right.

After this tragedy one of the most intensive shark hunts in history began. Hundreds of hunters scoured the area in boats. They used nets, they laid steel meshes across the creek and they fired thousands of rounds of ammunition into spots where sharks might be hiding. Hourly catches were made and many sharks writhing and threshing were dragged ashore.

Two days later, Michael Schleisser, a taxidermist, caught an eight-and-a-half-footer off South Amboy, New Jersey, about 4 miles north of Raritan Bay. When he opened the shark he found in its stomach a mass of flesh and bones weighing about 15 pounds. The bones were identified as human. They included portion of a shin bone which apparently belonged to Charles Bruder, who had been attacked nine days previously. Mr Schleisser mounted the skin and placed in on exhibit, where Dr J. T. Nichols, of the American Museum, saw it and positively identified the shark as the great white shark, *Carcharodon carcharias*.

After the capture of this killer, shark attacks ceased. Mr Murphy, of the Brooklyn Museum, and Dr Nichols investigated this remarkable series of tragedies and concluded that Schleisser's shark was a solitary one and the sole attacker of the men and boys.

There was no lack of theories to account for these killings. Some said it was a shark season. Others suggested the brute must have been suffering from a kind of shark rabies like a mad dog. There was another suggestion that owing to the interference with shipping – nobody had forgotten there was a world war on – the sharks missed the food they were used to getting from ocean liners and sought other victuals. There was a theory that recent naval disasters had given sharks an acquired taste for human flesh.

21

From *Sharks and Rays of Australian Seas*

David Stead

David Stead compiled the information in his book *Sharks and Rays of Australia,* in the early 1960s. Many of the accounts he so carefully documented regarding shark behaviour and attacks are no longer acceptable. For instance, a 15- to 20-foot grey nurse shark tossing its victim around like a cat torturing a mouse is, in the light of what we know about this species today, quite improbable. The shark was probably a light coloured great white, the only coldwater shark I know of who could have the strength to toss a human around on the surface. A very large grey nurse shark could possibly measure 12 feet in length, though I doubt that I have ever seen any longer than 10 feet and I have seen hundreds over the last twenty-one years.

I thought the secondhand account where Stead describes a massive sea creature, claiming it to be a shark, over 100 feet long very interesting. The crayfishermen in the area are even today a tough, no-nonsense bunch. Most are descendants of the old fishermen who started the industry at the turn of the century. If they came in and described to me a shark of immense length and girth, I would certainly be inclined to believe them.

We filmed a whale shark near Broughton Island. Perhaps the men were terrorized by an albino of the species. I saw a pilot whale once who was coloured a pale mottled cream, contrasting sharply with his black companion, so why not a mottled cream whale shark? We know so little about the sea and its inhabitants, working, as we do, only on the fringes of the ocean. Who can really know what great monsters lurk in the depths?

David Stead's book is full of interesting information about sharks and their close cousins, the rays. One thing that puzzles me, not only when reading Stead's book but also other similar publications, is the vast number of legs of pork that not only found their way into the ocean but were also eaten by sharks. It seems that, up to thirty years ago, pork was not only plentiful but not very expensive.

■

Though it is not my purpose in dealing with what might be termed as dangerous sharks, or those which may truly be regarded as potentially dangerous, in Australian waters, to give details of shark attacks, I shall be obliged to mention certain cases when considering the whaler shark. The only one I shall mention here in relation to the white pointer – as there was strong presumptive evidence that it was the species involved – is a shocking tragedy which occurred at Brighton, near Melbourne, in February 1930. Though, as I have said, the white pointer is more especially a pelagic species, it is not uncommon in its occurrence in the wide waters of Port Phillip and the lower areas of Hobart outer harbour.

At half past four in the afternoon of 15 February 1930, a lad who had just dived in off the end of the Middle Brighton Pier was seized by a very large shark – estimated in press statements variously to be from 15 to 20 feet in length – in full view of hundreds of people who had gathered for an interstate sailing race. The shark dragged him down out of sight momentarily, and then he was seen again for an instant, apparently still in the grip of the shark as it swam out into the deeper water and disappeared with its human prey. Although search parties went out immediately to look for the lad's body, and continued the search in the days following, while the water was dragged for a great distance around, no trace of him was ever found. It was stated authoritatively at the time that this was the first shark tragedy in the locality for fifty-four years. Piecing together some of the eyewitnesses' accounts and discussing the matter with them on the spot later, I came to the conclusion that the monster was a great shark, probably about 18 to 20 feet long. The carrying of the body right away is quite an unusual feature of shark tragedies – with which, sadly enough, we have been only too familiar in our east coast waters, notably in the vicinity of Sydney and Newcastle.

I have mentioned this instance particularly because, however black the record of the White Death may be in the waters of the world beyond Australia, as I have previously indicated we have very little in the way of attacks on humans to pin on the monster. Nor in this case could the shark be identified with any certainty, as the flurry in the water prevented any observer from seeing it clearly.

The brief account that I have given of this shocking occurrence is founded upon the personal evidence of eyewitnesses who talked to me shortly after the tragedy. As is well known, press accounts frequently contain lurid exaggerations of these shark attacks, and are sometimes filled with fanciful details not noted by careful observers. There were several such accounts in some of the Australian newspapers relating to this Brighton attack. Dr Schultz, in his excellent book *The Ways of Fishes* (1948), has introduced an account of the Brighton occurrence which, unfortunately, reads like one of these fanciful newspaper statements. I hasten to add that Dr Schultz is well known to me as a careful and competent ichthyologist, who would not willingly lend himself to sensational journalism. Here is his account:

> In 1930 an eighteen-year-old youth, bathing at Melbourne, Australia, was cruelly murdered by an enormous grey nurse shark, estimated to be 15 to 20 feet long. The fish seized its screaming victim in its huge jaws, gripped him at the waist with its sharp teeth, submerged him and emerged again ten times, tossing him about like a cat torturing a mouse. Each time the animal and the youth appeared above water, they were further down the bay, leaving a bloody trail. The scream became fainter and fainter and ultimately the shark carried its victim off and down for the last time.

It will be remembered that, in discussing some records as to the size attained by the white pointer in various seas, I said that there had been quite trustworthy accounts on the New South Wales coast indicating the existence of much larger sharks than those mentioned. The most extraordinary of these I shall relate. The first, is not so hard to swallow! But as for the second...!

In May 1939, during some discussions in the Sydney press regarding the stature of sharks, Captain J. S. Elkington of Queensland wrote to me to tell me of an observation that he made in the year 1894 of a great shark outside Townsville Breakwater. (I may mention that Captain Elkington spent a considerable part of his life in the service of the sea, and was always a keen observer of Nature.) He said that while the 35-foot launch he was in was broken down for half an hour this shark lay within ten feet of the launch, giving him ample opportunity for observation. 'It was not a basker, (basking shark),' he wrote, 'but a real white or yellowish sort, which projected a couple of feet at least beyond each end of the launch.' This observer knew the basking shark and was sure that the one seen was the great white shark.

The second account that I shall give is regarded by me as the most outstanding of all stories relating to the gigantic forms of this fish that has ever come to light – I mean, of course, accounts which really appeared to be founded upon fact. In the year 1918 I recorded the sensation that had been caused among the 'outside' crayfish men at Port Stephens, when, for several days, they refused to go to sea to their regular fishing grounds in the vicinity of Broughton Island. The men had been at work on the fishing grounds – which lie in deep water – when an immense shark of almost unbelievable proportions put in an appearance, lifting pot after pot containing many crayfishes, and taking, as the men said, 'pots, mooring lines and all.' These crayfish pots, it should be mentioned, were about 3 feet 6 inches in diameter and frequently contained from two to three dozen good-sized crayfish each weighing several pounds. The men were all unanimous that this shark was something the like of which they had never dreamed of. In company with the local fisheries inspector I questioned many of the men very closely and they all agreed as to the gigantic stature of the beast. But the lengths they gave were, on the whole, absurd. I mention them, however, as an indication of the state of mind which this unusual giant had thrown them into. And bear in mind that these were men who were used to the sea and all sorts of weather, and all sorts of sharks as well. One of the crew said the shark was 'three hundred feet long at least'! Others said it was as long as the wharf on which we stood – about 115 feet! They affirmed that the water 'boiled' over a large space when the fish swam past. They were all familiar with whales, which they had often seen passing at sea, but this was a vast shark. They had seen its terrible head which was 'at least as large as the roof of the wharf shed at Nelson's Bay.' Impossible, of course! But these were prosaic and rather stolid men, not given to 'fish stories' nor even to talking at all about their catches. Further, they knew that the person they were talking to (myself) had heard all the fish stories years before! One of the things that impressed me was that they all agreed as to the ghostly whitish colour of the vast fish. The local fisheries inspector of the time, Mr Paton, agreed with me that it must have been something really gigantic to put these experienced men into such a state of fear and panic.

Personally I have little doubt that in this occurrence we had one of those very rare occasions when humans have been vouchsafed a glimpse of one of those enormous sharks of the White Death type which we know to exist, or to have existed in the recent past, in the depths of the sea. While they are probably not abundant they may yet be so. Lest the reader may still think me to be credulous I would like to say that I have seen actual teeth of a shark of this type which were no less than five inches (individually) across the base. They had been dredged up from the bottom of the Pacific Ocean. These, I believe, were not fossil teeth, such as are found in various tertiary deposits – from which large quantities of great teeth of the white shark type have been obtained. In my opinion they were so recent as to justify the belief that they had come from great sharks of a type which might still exist in the deep seas! Such a shark as that might readily take the whole of a crayfish man's outfit – pots, crayfish, lines and boat! A shark possessing such teeth would be from 80 to 90 feet long.

22

From *The Shark Arm Case*

Vince Kelly

There are few Australians who haven't heard of the shark arm murder case. It has been a standby on the historical feature pages for years. It was a classic case of thieves falling out.

It hasn't anything to do with sharks at all, other than the fact that somehow a shark swallowed an arm belonging to a murdered man. The rest of the body was never recovered, nor was his killer brought to justice.

The murdered man's name was James Smith. The police reconstructed the crime in this way: Smith's body was probably cut up by his murderer. The parts of the body were placed in a tin trunk, which was completely filled without the arm. Unable to get this in, the murderer cut it off and attached it to the outside of the trunk with rope, tying one end of the rope round the wrist. The trunk and its contents were then taken out to sea and dumped. The arm worked loose and was swallowed by a shark.

At the inquest following identification of the victim, expert witnesses, one of whom was Dr Coppleson, who later published a book on shark attacks, testified that they thought that the arm was removed with a knife, not torn off in a shark attack, even though the arm had wounds caused by a shark's teeth on it.

■

The chain of events leading to the sensational explanation for James Smith's disappearance began in a humdrum fashion. On 27 April Bert Hobson was in his boat a mile and a half off Coogee Beach. He left a set line there after baiting it for shark with mackerel.

Next day he found he had caught not one shark but two. A small one was just being devoured by a 14-foot tiger shark which had tangled itself in the line … Bert Hobson towed the catch to the beach, where it was quickly transferred to his brother's aquarium as the star attraction. Captive sharks have a macabre fascination for a city of surf lovers and the 14-foot tiger attracted crowds daily.

The aquarium proprietor, Charles Hobson, was pleased. He fed the shark on mackerel, but after the first four days it rejected food and wallowed sullenly in the water.

Bert Hobson was among the crowd watching its sluggish manoeuvres at 4:30 on the afternoon of Anzac Day, the seventh day of its captivity. Like the others, he was intrigued when the shark suddenly began to surge violently about the tank as though demented.

When it disgorged pieces of rats, birds and fins, and a human arm, Bert Hobson's shouts brought his brother, Charles, who promptly phoned Randwick police station to report the gruesome find.

Detective Frank Head and Constable John Mannion got there at 4:45. Bert Hobson was still guarding the arm. Warily, his eye on the shark, Head hauled it out with a firm grip on a piece of rope. It was tied tightly about the wrist with two half-hitches. On the forearm was a tattoo of two boxers shaping up at each other. They were tattooed in blue-inked outlines, their shorts in red. For everyone who knew James Smith the arm was the answer to the mystery of his disappearance. But the police were wasting no time in attempting to establish beyond doubt the identity of the arm's owner. Constable John Lindsay had been rushed from the fingerprint section of the CIB. The fingerprint impressions from the skin removed by Constable Lindsay were blurred in the case of most of the fingers, but those from the thumb and ring finger were found to match those in the police records in the name of James Smith.

The comparison was made by the fingerprint expert, Detective Ewing, and he satisfied himself of this beyond any doubt. The earlier prints had been taken and recorded by Constable Masters, of Balmain, in September, 1932, after police had raided Smith's Rozelle Sports Club and charged him with illegal betting.

Smith was convicted of the charge. It was not a very important crime, but that raid yielded fingerprints to support the evidence of the tattooed boxers that the arm belonged to the missing James Smith.

To Smith's brother, Edward, a Newtown rope maker, the additional evidence of the fingerprints was unnecessary. After reading the account of the finding of the arm and the description of the tattooed boxers he called at Newtown Police Station. He said there was no doubt in his mind that the arm was that of his brother Jim, who had been missing since 8 April.

Edward Smith then called at the Gladesville home to talk the matter over with his brother's wife – or widow. She was with his mother-in-law, Mrs Johanna Molloy.

In the family conference Smith's distressed relatives compared notes on when they had last seen him. They were all agreed that he appeared unworried and in the best of health.

Gladys Smith recalled that she had not seen her husband since 7 April. He had escorted her to the tram stop at about nine o'clock that evening when she was leaving her home for a few days.

He had expected to go on a fishing trip before she left – 'to drive Greg Vaughan and a party at 5 pounds a week.' When she asked him why he hadn't gone she said he replied that they hadn't sent the money for his fare.

Her mother related that he had left home on 8 April. On that morning she had heard him talking to a small boy at the front gate. She had not actually seen the boy, but she had heard their voices. When the boy had gone Smith came into the house and said he would be going fishing.

Mrs Molloy said, 'He told me they had sent the money for his fare this time and you weren't to worry. He left here about half-past nine that morning. He said he was to meet a man of independent means from another State.'

Mrs Molloy added that she had told him, 'You be careful, Jimmy,' and he replied cheerfully, 'I'll be careful, Mum.'

Edward Smith's recollection was that Jim had urged him to accompany him on the fishing excursion, but Edward was not anxious to go. He said he had told his brother, 'I'm not keen on going fishing with strangers.'

But there was another date discussed at the family conference. This was recalled by both Gladys and Edward Smith. The date was 13 April.

It is important because what happened that day tried to make it appear that James Smith was still alive at least five days after police were to allege that he had been murdered by Patrick Brady, his close friend and fellow conspirator in a scheme to commit robberies by forgery.

It was one of two messages clearly intended to mislead investigations by police. On that date a neighbour relayed a telephone message to Gladys Smith. 13 April was a Saturday. The message was to the effect that her husband would not be back until the following Monday, and she was not to worry.

Gladys Smith remembered it. Her son, Raymond, eighteen, remembered it because he passed it on to his Uncle Edward in the Queen's Hotel, Enmore, on the same afternoon. He told his uncle, 'Mum just got a telephone message to say Dad won't be home till Monday.

Edward Smith's comment had been, 'That's funny. He knows where to find me, but he never let me know. Something must have happened.'

His premonition of disaster was more soundly based than he imagined, but it was not shared by his sister-in-law, who allowed another week to elapse before she initiated personal inquiries about her missing husband. On 20 April she phoned the Hotel Cecil, Cronulla, but was told only that he had been seen 'about the place' a few days earlier.

Gladys Smith telephoned Vaughan on 24 April – the day before the shark disgorged her husband's arm – and told him she had heard nothing from her husband for more than a fortnight. She had then asked him bluntly, 'What's wrong with Jimmy?'

When Vaughan said he didn't know what she was talking about, she had been incredulous and said, 'You're joking, aren't you?'

'No, Mrs Smith, I'm not joking,' replied Vaughan. 'I don't know what you mean. He wasn't going fishing with me, but Jimmy did come here before he went to Cronulla. He said he was taking a boat or something to Cronulla.'

These were the days of ordeal of Gladys Smith. She was taken to the morgue where she had to face the unnerving sight of the tattooed arm, which the stricken woman positively identified as her husband's.

The Government Medical Officer, Dr Aubrey Palmer, had examined the limb at the morgue on the day after it was taken from the aquarium. Because of the report that it had been bitten from a body by a shark, he had specially requested his friend, Dr Victor Coppleson, to inspect it with him. Dr Coppleson was an accepted authority on sharks.

In evidence, Dr Palmer was to say later that on 26 April 1935, he made an examination of a left upper arm identified to him by Constable Mannion at the City Morgue.

'I made a preliminary examination with Dr Coppleson, later it was taken away. When I made an examination a piece of rope was attached to it. It was tight on the wrist, with an ordinary clove hitch. The arm had been disarticulated at the shoulder joint, a more or less circular incision.

Police Prosecutor Sergeant William Toole asked, 'From your examination of the skin of the arm did you form any opinion whether a sharp instrument had been used to remove it?'

DR PALMER: Yes. A fairly sharp instrument I think.

SGT TOOLE: And the cartilage covering the bone?

DR PALMER: The cartilage covering the head of the bone had several scratches. A number of scratches and one small cut. The cartilage was soft in one place too.

SGT TOOLE: Were there any other wounds on the arm?

DR PALMER: Above the elbow in front there was a transverse wound five inches long. That is the wound showing above the elbow. For a good part it was fairly clean cut and in other parts more ragged. I think the raggedness was due to changes taking place after death.

SGT. TOOLE: Was the arm in a good state of preservation?

DR PALMER: Comparatively a fair state of preservation. It had some smell of decomposition. The cut on the shoulder was fairly clean.

At the first examination Dr Coppleson was with me. Constable Raines signed for and took the limb and the limb was later returned to me.

SGT TOOLE: Later did you submit the bulk of the soft tissues of the arm to the Government Analyst?

DR PALMER: Yes, the report from the Government Analyst showed no chemical preservation had been used to preserve the arm. And I thought also that it was unlikely that the person to whom the arm had belonged had died from poison, or at any rate from more common poisons.

SGT TOOLE: From your dissection of the arm did you arrive at any conclusion as to how the arm had been removed?

DR PALMER: I took it that the arm had been removed from the body by a fairly sharp instrument.

SGT TOOLE: Would you say it was done by a surgeon?

DR PALMER: It was obviously not done by a surgeon. There were no flaps left. It was obviously not done by a surgeon in an operation.

SGT TOOLE: Did you form any opinion as to whether the arm came from a living person or a dead body?

DR PALMER: I would not be absolutely certain that it came from a dead body, owing to the changes that took place. The difficulty of deciding is largely due to the changes that took place after death partly owing to decomposition and partly possibly owing to digestion. But I could not conceive that the person from whom the arm was taken was alive, or still alive at any rate.

SGT TOOLE: Did you notice if there was any blood in the tissues?

DR PALMER: There was no blood effused, thrown out, in the tissues at the cut edges, but there was a little blood in the different vessels and through the limbs, in the nature of clots.

SGT TOOLE: Did you form any opinion as to how long the arm had been removed from the body?

DR PALMER: Not exactly; not more than a few weeks at any rate. An arm keeps better when severed from the body. It might be some weeks. But it is impossible to tell exactly.

SGT TOOLE: Would it be possible for a man to remove his arm himself in the manner in which you found it?

DR PALMER: I think it extremely unlikely that a man could remove it himself. It is not a thing he could do with one sweep, although it is remarkable what terrible wounds some people, lunatics, do inflict on themselves.

SGT TOOLE: Have you had any experience in connection with the digestion of sharks?

DR PALMER: Not personally but through the courtesy of Dr Dakin, Professor of Zoology at Sydney University, I have learned a little.

SGT TOOLE: From that did you arrive at any opinion as to a shark's digestion?

DR PALMER: Yes. It is a cold-blooded animal and the digestion is slow, more especially in cold water. Sometimes they starve for some time and then when they have a feed it takes some time to digest, from days to weeks.

SGT TOOLE: If the arm had been swallowed by a small shark and the small shark swallowed by a large shark, would that have any effect on the arm?

DR PALMER: No doubt the digestion would be slower. There would be a certain amount of shark digested first, although there might be some digestive juices left in the swallowed shark. But I should think that there would not be much digestion by the swallowed shark, so the swallowed shark would have to be digested first. But in any case, there would not be anything unusual about an arm remaining in a shark for a week without being digested.

Dr Palmer said that on 13 June he saw Mrs Smith at the City Morgue in the presence of the City Coroner, Mr Evatt and Sergeant Toole and showed her two pieces of skin, with the tattoo marks on them. She told him what she expected to see if they belonged to her husband.

SGT TOOLE: Have you the pieces of skin with you?

DR PALMER: I have them, but I do not usually produce dead bodies, or parts of dead bodies, unless the court ask me to do so.

The two pieces of skin were tendered and marked for exhibit.

Dr Palmer said that he had later read a treatise by a German professor, Dr Ernest Weinhart, which appeared in *Zeitschrift fur Biologie*.

Mr Clive Evatt, the barrister briefed for Brady, asked him, 'Relying on this thesis of the German doctor I suppose you agree that it is conceivable that if as much of the human arm as existed in this case, if it were torn or cut off the trunk, that the individual could survive?'

DR PALMER: That is so, I agree.

MR EVATT: If met in train accidents, machinery and factory?

Again Dr Palmer agreed that the evidence he relied on principally was 'the state of the arm, that it came off after death.'

MR EVATT: Again there is grave difficulty on account of the fact that it would be on those portions that the digestive juices would commence to work?

DR PALMER: That is so, and decomposition, too.

Dr Palmer said he had discarded the possibility of poisoning. Had the person died of some of our well-known poisons at any rate, he would have expected to find traces.

Mr Evatt was sticking to his trump card. An amputated limb did not prove its owner dead.

MR EVATT: There are two conclusions that I put to you; that there is no evidence available as to how the man died, that is, assuming he is dead, and secondly, the individual from whom the arm came could still be alive today?

DR PALMER: I would not deny the possibility, but I could hardly conceive that he would be.

Dr Palmer's evidence was followed by that of Dr Victor Marcus Coppleson, with whom shark fishing and observation was almost a lifetime study. He was also a wealthy specialist and resided in one of Sydney's exclusive suburbs, Point Piper. He told the court that he identified the arm and made an examination of it. He said it had been removed by a sharp instrument at the shoulder joint.

Sergeant Toole asked him, 'Did you form an opinion as to whether it had been removed by a surgeon or otherwise?'

DR COPPLESON: I formed the opinion that it had not been removed by a surgeon. In the first place, there were no flaps actually cut.

SGT TOOLE: Did you form any opinion as to whether it had been removed from a living being or a dead body?

DR COPPLESON: My examination was mainly from the surgical aspect and I formed the opinion from such evidence as there was. My chief point was not so much as to whether it was removed before or after death. Such evidence as there was appeared to show it was removed after death.

Mr Evatt was still shrewdly adhering to the theory that Smith's tattooed arm did not prove that Smith was murdered or even dead. He asked Dr Coppleson, 'Your chief interest was to ascertain whether the arm was bitten off by a shark?'

DR COPPLESON: I don't know. Dr Palmer rang me and told me that he had an arm down there and he would like me to come down.

MR EVATT: Dr Palmer regarded you as having experience in shark bites at St Vincent's Hospital?

DR COPPLESON: Not necessarily at St Vincent's. He knows I am interested in shark bites. I have seen shark bites at the morgue with Dr Palmer.

MR EVATT: You consider it was not a shark bite, neither that on the shoulder or on the arm?

DR COPPLESON: There was evidence that this arm had been bitten in parts by a shark. There was evidence of shark's teeth marks on the forearm. On the back of the arm there were small marks which appeared to have been made by a shark's teeth. There were a number of small triangular marks...

MR EVATT: What about this mark (showing on the photograph)?

DR COPPLESON: I cannot remember that exactly, I would not say whether it was or was not. The wound over the elbow – there is some doubt whether that was caused by a knife or by a shark bite.

MR EVATT: You agree that it is impossible to say definitely whether the arm came from a dead or a living person?

DR COPPLESON: At the time of removal? I am of the opinion that it did come from a dead body, but I would not say for certain.

MR EVATT: You did say that it was impossible to say for certain whether the arm was cut from a dead or living person?

DR COPPLESON: That is so.

MR EVATT: You agree generally with the conclusions that I put to Dr Palmer: That the arm itself in no way revealed how death eventuated, assuming that the person is now dead from whom the arm came, either before or after death?

DR COPPLESON: If it came from a dead body, there is no evidence how that person died.

MR EVATT: Suppose it had been cut off by a machine?

DR COPPLESON: That is different. A machine tears the arm off ... pulls it off.

MR EVATT: And in other cases it is cut off?

DR COPPLESON: I can't say that I have heard of a person living after that. But in a tearing injury it is possible that a person might live. In a tearing the arteries react differently.

MR EVATT: I am putting it as a theory.

DR COPPLESON: With immediate attention, a person could survive, provided the arteries and vessels are tied ...

MR EVATT: Have you ever known an arm to be torn off by a shark in that manner?

DR COPPLESON: Yes, in the Sydney Hospital. A boy there had his arm taken off at the shoulder. The boy died.

Both doctors agreed that the arm appeared to have been severed with a knife or some blade instrument rather than a shark bite although they noted scars on the forearm and accepted them as wounds caused by teeth of a shark.

But were they? Quite a different explanation for them would have been claimed by the defence had Patrick Brady's trial for murder not been halted by the judge with his direction to the jury to acquit Brady.

Acknowledgements

Grateful acknowledgement is made for permission to use the selections included in this anthology, as follows:

From *Blue Meridian* by Peter Matthiessen. Copyright © 1971 Peter Matthiessen. Reprinted by permission of Random House, Inc., and Candida Donadio & Associates, Inc.

From *Jaws* by Peter Benchley. Copyright © 1974 Peter Benchley. Reprinted by permission of Doubleday & Company, Inc. and Andre Deutsch Limited.

From *Sharks, Sea and Land* by 'Sinbad,' published by Blackfriars Printing & Publishing Co., 1889.

From *Lord of the Sharks* by Franco Prosperi, translated by Camilla and Guido Roatta, published by the Hutchinson Publishing Group.

The Vanishing Grey Nurse by Valerie Taylor, reprinted from *The Australian Women's Weekly* by permission of the author.

From *The Arcturus Adventure* by William Beebe. Copyright 1926 William Beebe; renewed 1954 by William Beebe. Reprinted by permission of G. P. Putnam's Sons.

From *Sharks and Other Ancestors* by Wade Doak, published by Hodder & Stoughton, Auckland, N.Z. Copyright © 1975 Wade Doak. Reprinted by permission of the author and the publisher.

'Sharks That Ring Bells' from *The Lady and the Sharks* by Eugenie Clark. Copyright © 1969 Eugenie Clark. Reprinted by permission of Harper & Row, Publishers, Inc.

From *The Coast of Coral* by Arthur C. Clarke. Copyright © 1956 Arthur Charles Clarke. Reprinted by permission of Harper & Row, Publishers. Inc., and David Higham Associates Limited.

From *Men Beneath the Sea: Conquest of the Underwater World* by Hans Hass. Copyright © 1975 Hans Hass. Reprinted by permission of St. Martin's Press, Inc. and David & Charles Ltd.

'The Great Shark of Jurien Bay' from *Sharks and Shipwrecks* by Hugh Edwards, published by Landsdowne Press, Sydney, and Quadrangle / The New York Times Book Co., New York. Copyright © 1975 Hugh Edwards. Reprinted by permission of the author.

From *Shark Attack* by H. David Baldridge. Published by Berkley Publishing Corp., New York, 1975. Copyright © 1974 H. David Baldridge. Reprinted by permission of the author.

From *About Sharks and Shark Attack* edited by David H. Davies. Copyright © 1964 David H. Davies. Reprinted by permission of Routledge & Kegan Paul Ltd.

From *Shark Attack* by Victor M. Coppleson. Copyright © 1958 Victor Coppleson, © 1968 Enid Coppleson. Reprinted by permission of Angus and Robertson Publishers, Sydney. (This book was reprinted in 1976 under the title *Killer Sharks*.)

From *Sharks and Rays of Australian Seas* by David Stead. Copyright © 1963 by Thistle Stead. Reprinted by permission of Angus and Robertson Publishers, Sydney.

From *The Shark Arm Case* by Vince Kelly. Copyright © 1963 Vince Kelly. Reprinted by permission of Angus and Robertson Publishers, Sydney.